William Leonard Parsons

Satan's Devices and the Believer's Victory

William Leonard Parsons

Satan's Devices and the Believer's Victory

ISBN/EAN: 9783337309091

Printed in Europe, USA, Canada, Australia, Japan

Cover: Foto ©Lupo / pixelio.de

More available books at **www.hansebooks.com**

SATAN'S DEVICES

AND THE

BELIEVER'S VICTORY.

BY

REV. WM. L. PARSONS, A. M.,

PASTOR OF THE CONGREGATIONAL CHURCH, MATTAPOISETT, MASS.

Lest Satan should get an advantage of us; for we are not ignorant of his devices.
2 Cor. 2:11.
And the God of peace shall bruise Satan under your feet shortly. Rom. 16:20.

BOSTON:
PUBLISHED BY THE AUTHOR.
1864.

PREFACE.

To comprehend the forces which resist one's progress in any right direction, is a most important study — an essential condition of success. To know our enemy, — how, when, where, and with what weapons he will attack us, — goes far to insure a victory.

This principle applies, in all its force, in spiritual matters. We have, in the Christian warfare, relentless and most artful foes to contend with; and, if we would not "beat the air," and be shamefully driven from the field, we must know our enemy, in his tactics and in his defenses, and how we may effectually use against him those weapons which are "mighty through God to the pulling down of strongholds." A successful reconnoissance of the foe is half the battle.

If this volume has any merit, it lies, in the author's judgment, in this: **that** it brings the opposing forces which are at work, on the one hand, to destroy, and, on the other, to save the soul, into an open field, face to face; that it exposes the enemy at his work of death, so that he can be seen and understood, and so that the powers of the gospel may be *intelligently* and *effectually* brought to bear against him, till the "prey of the terrible shall be delivered."

The work aims to be a sort of "hand-book" for all who would "fight the good fight of faith," whether they have or have not, yet entered upon the duty; whether they are in the infancy or childhood of the spiritual life, or whether they have made the highest attainments known among the saints. It seeks to meet the wants of men of all denominations, or of none, who hope to reach heaven through the redemption of Christ; to make the way clear from Egypt to the Land of Promise; and to show how to enter the land and gather its precious fruits. The things it attempts to present are as needful to be known, and well known, both to the Christian and to him who would be such, as the fundamental rules of arithmetic, to the **mathematician**.

The chapter on the subject of Sanctification aims to give a more complete and satisfactory view than would easily be gained from writers who have presented only some specific phases of that doctrine. The author entertains the hope that he has presented it from a stand-point from which all Christians will be able to see eye to eye, in respect to it, and to be quickened to lay hold of "the fullness of the blessing of the gospel of Christ." The chapter contains, in its last section, some applications of principles which may afford some light to the popular mind, on certain vexed questions in theology.

Various "pastor's sketches" are introduced, which, it is hoped, will make clear some of the more essential and difficult points, and help to fix them in the memory.

The work contains no learned disquisitions concerning the existence or nature of Satan. Its object is entirely practical, and its teachings will be found scarcely less important to those who deny, than to those who admit, his personal existence. The author has followed the simple method of the Bible, and has felt authorized, wherever he has found lies doing their fatal work, to charge their fatherhood upon Satan; and so on, through all the catalogue of abominations ascribed to him in the Scriptures.

It is needless to say that nothing is claimed for the work as a mere literary performance. The object of the writer has been to communicate, in a simple way, a kind of instruction, the great need of which in the churches, his own ministry — spent somewhat largely in revivals of religion — has made him deeply and painfully feel.

The author would be most happy to have each of its readers regard the work as affectionately dedicated to himself, and to have it read with that peculiar interest which is awakened by a conscious personal friendship existing between author and reader.

CONTENTS.

	PAGE
CHAPTER I. Introductory.—The Case stated.—Its Application to those who do and those who do not profess Christianity.	11
CHAPTER II. Personal Existence of Satan.—Bible View presented.—Objections answered.	15
CHAPTER III. Character of Satan.	21
CHAPTER IV. The Battle Field surveyed.—The Human Mind and its Principles of Action.	24
CHAPTER V. What must be Satan's Methods of Working, as indicated by the Changeless Laws of our Mental and Moral Constitutions.	33
CHAPTER VI. Primary Importance to the Christian Life of the Right Adjustment of the Will to the Truth, illustrated by a "Pastor's Sketch."	37
CHAPTER VII. Satan, the "Author and Finisher" of Unbelief.	44
CHAPTER VIII. Satan, in the Height of his Power, obscuring the Essential Object of Faith, Christ Jesus the Lord; thus rendering impossible the Exercise of a Living Faith.	48
CHAPTER IX. Satan's Second Eclipse of the Object of Faith—hiding also the Deity of the Spirit, and for a Like Purpose.	55

CHAPTER X. The Mischiefs Satan accomplishes by removing from before the Eye of Faith the Godhead of Christ and the Spirit. 60

CHAPTER XI. Satan, sowing Tares. — Pastor's Sketch illustrating the Necessity of having the Right Seed-Truth sown in the Heart, that a True Christian Character may grow therefrom. 64

CHAPTER XII. Satan, as the Father of Lies. — Principles premised. 1. His Object is to destroy the Soul. 2. Lies received are held *as Truths*, and thus they have all the Binding Force of Truth and all the Damaging Effect of Lies. 3. They exclude Corresponding Truths from the Mind. 4. To receive them Involves an Impeachment of the Divine Character. 5. They are anchored primarily in the *Sensibility*, not in the Reason. 6. They are adapted to meet the Idiosyncrasies and Prejudices of Men. 7. Language is not required to express them. 8. When thoroughly lodged in the Mind, it is difficult, and often impossible, to remove them. 70

CHAPTER XIII. The Lies whereby Satan keeps Men from becoming Christians. 74

CHAPTER XIV. The Lies by which Satan aims to weaken and waste the Inner Life of Christians. 86

CHAPTER XV. The Fiery Darts of the Wicked One, illustrated by a Sketch of a Remarkable Case. 101

CHAPTER XVI. Satan, as the "Accuser of the Brethren." . 108

CHAPTER XVII. Wherein Satan is considered as the Tempter. 113

CHAPTER XVIII. Wherein appears the Christian's Deliverer. — Method of Victory shown. 121

CHAPTER XIX. Satan, as transformed into an Angel of Light. — Pastor's Sketches. 132

CHAPTER XX. How to distinguish between Satan, so transformed into an Angel of Light, and Christ, the True Angel and Messenger of God, whom Satan counterfeits. 146

CHAPTER XXI. Satanic Plots. — Pastor's Sketch. . . . 159

CHAPTER XXII. Satan, the Enemy of Prayer and Vital Communion with God. 168

CHAPTER XXIII. Satan, as Philosopher, Theologian, and Logician. 180

CHAPTER XXIV. The Allies of Satan. 201

CHAPTER XXV. Satan, the Foe of our Sanctification and Growth in Grace. 209

Section 1. Theories of the Different Schools considered, and shown to differ only in Speculative, not Essential Points. 210

Section 2. All Attainments in the Divine Life the Result of knowing God in the Heart. 213

Section 3. This Knowledge the Exclusive Gift of the Spirit — its Positive and Assuring Nature. 218

Section 4. Conditions of receiving this Life-giving Knowledge of God. — A Theological Difficulty met. . 223

Section 5. The Relations of Revealed Truth to our Growing Sanctification. 226

Section 6. The Relation between knowing God by the Spirit, and the Enjoyment of the Life of Holiness. . . 228

Section 7. The Natural and Life-giving Effect upon the Mind of knowing, from Heaven, certain Definite Things concerning God and ourselves — concerning his Relations to us and ours to him. 229

Section 8. The Law of Progress in this Divine, Saving Knowledge; with a Sketch illustrating the Spirit's Method. — The "Higher Christian Life" explained. . 241

Section 9. What may we reasonably hope to attain in this Life, in Respect to the State, (1.) Of the Will;

(2.) Of the Intellect; (3.) Of the Sensibility;—or in the Matter of Purpose, Knowledge, and Emotion? . . . 251

Section 10. The Relation of Faith to the Obtaining of this Saving Knowledge of God. 259

Section 11. The Duty of Living in the Victorious Enjoyment of this Life-sustaining Knowledge of God. 261

Section 12. The Guilt of being without this Knowledge and its Saving Power. 264

Section 13. The General View here presented, confirmed by its Power to harmonize the apparently Conflicting Views of the Different Schools of Evangelical Christians, and to simplify certain Vexed Questions in Theology. 267

CHAPTER XXVI. Satan's Methods of Opposing the Christian's Sanctification. 281

CHAPTER XXVII. Satan's Efforts to Cripple the Ministers of the Gospel, and render their Preaching powerless. . . 294

CHAPTER XXVIII. The Great Fight with and Victory over Satan; with a Pastor's Sketch of the Battle Scene. . . 302

SATAN'S DEVICES

AND

THE BELIEVER'S VICTORY.

CHAPTER I.

INTRODUCTORY.—THE CASE STATED.—ITS APPLICATION TO THOSE WHO DO AND THOSE WHO DO NOT PROFESS CHRISTIANITY.

Prove all things; hold fast that which is good.—1 *Thess.* 5: 21.

IF the numerous engines which daily leave the depot of any of our great central railroads, after proceeding a short distance, should run from the track, causing great loss of property and life; if, on coming to a moderate up-grade, they should fail to draw the trains; if their movements were spasmodic, sometimes violent, and, as frequently almost suspended; if they exhibited a strange propensity to leave the rails and make for the carriage road; if, in short, they failed to obey the will of the engineer,—the causes of such perverted action would be forthwith searched out and removed.

It evidently does come to pass, that many who are hopefully converted to Christ, soon after leaving the depot for their heavenly destination, do strangely leave the track; they fail on the up-grades of duty; their movements are irregular; the wheels of their faith slip on the rails of promise; they do not promptly obey the will of the Divine Engineer. It is the sore grief of the ministry and church, and the general complaint and stumbling-block of the world, that professed Christians fall so far below the standard of character presented in the Bible — that they so manifestly fail in running the Christian race. Christ proclaims liberty, and yet many of his people are slaves to the world and their lusts. The gospel professes to open fountains in the desert, and rivers in dry places; and yet we fail to find "the rivers, the floods, the brooks of honey and butter," of which Zophar the Naamathite writes (Job 20:17), and drink, instead, at those transient streams of which Job himself speaks, which dry up and vanish when the heat comes, and go to nothing (6: 15–18). We lack the "tongue of fire," the baptism of the Spirit, "the fullness of the blessing of the gospel of Christ." And the worst of all is, that the church is extensively paralyzed with the fatal idea that this state of bondage and spiritual weakness is practically incurable; and, as the inevitable consequence, men abandon themselves to a current of most unsatisfactory and bewildering experiences.

The subject has its application to unconverted men. They know they are involved in sin, and must be redeemed from it or be lost. The only way to heaven is over the highway of holiness (Isa. 35 : 8–10), which the Lord has ordered to be graded (Isa. 62 : 10), for his ransomed to pass over. They see, with somewhat distorted vision, the failures and inconsistencies of Christians, and therefore reject the only possible way of salvation—that provided by the atonement of Christ. They are not going to commit the ridiculous figure of running from the track, or of failing on the up-grades of temptation, and so propose to reach the heavenly destination without passing over the only road which leads thither.

The majority of professed Christians are evidently in such bondage that they can not use their powers in the service of Christ with the same happy freedom and efficiency which they exhibit in the affairs of every day life; they are little less than prisoners of war; and the mass of unconverted men look upon the whole subject of experimental Christianity as involved in a mystery they can not understand, and therefore dismiss it as having no valid claims upon them.

Here is a state of things which ought not to exist. In its production, we believe Satan has a most subtle agency and a prodigious power. There are many, who, in general, admit this, but who do not see clearly *how* he accomplishes his malignant purposes.

They have little hope of being able to understand his methods so as to escape his devices; and their state of mind amounts to a surrender to the adversary. To many others, not a few in the churches probably, Satan is a myth; and such he leads " captive at his will" with scarce an attempt, on their part, at resistance.

We believe this great enemy of God and of man can be successfully exposed, so that men may escape his ruinous devices. This is the work we shall attempt in the following chapters.

Satan, as the grand disorganizer of the "system of the universe," we will leave to Dr. Edward Beecher, aiming only to expose those malignant processes by which he seeks to destroy the individual soul.

CHAPTER II.

PERSONAL EXISTENCE OF SATAN.—BIBLE VIEW PRESENTED. OBJECTIONS ANSWERED.

And the great dragon was cast out, that old serpent, called the Devil and Satan, which deceiveth the whole world; he was cast out into the earth, and his angels were cast out with him.— Rev. 12 : 9.

As to the origin of Satan, the Scriptures give us no extended account. We have the testimony of Peter (2 Pet. 2 : 4), that certain of the angels of God sinned, and were cast down from heaven, and delivered into chains of darkness to be reserved unto judgment, when they are to be finally doomed to the lake of fire. This company of fallen spirits are represented as in the earth, moving up and down among its inhabitants to deceive men and destroy their souls. Their chief is revealed in the Bible by a great variety of names, which imply his personal existence. He is often called Satan, which means an enemy or adversary; the Devil, from a Greek word meaning to calumniate; or from two words signifying without light, making this name nearly synonymous with "Prince of darkness;" the Father of lies, which, in some sense, implies that all the falsehoods ever devised in the world are of his coining; a murderer, which indicates his agency in every murder since the days of Cain; the Tempter; Beelzebub; the Accuser of the brethren; the God and Prince of this world; Lucifer; Serpent; Tormentor; Roaring lion; in Hebrew, Abaddon; in Greek, Apollyon, meaning destroyer. Such are some of the names by which the Scriptures designate the being of whom we write.

Satan thus stands out upon the inspired page as a personal being, a conscious, emotional, voluntary individuality, as much so as Paul or Christ. Archbishop Whately could employ his genius to discredit the personal existence of Satan no more successfully than he did to disprove that of Napoleon. The Bible every where treats him as a great commanding, ruling, and powerful spirit. Christ was accused of casting out devils by Beelzebub, the chief of the devils (Luke 11 : 15). The supremacy of Satan among fallen spirits is recognized whenever they are classed together as "the devil and his angels." He is represented as the "god of this world," ruling it as a sovereign to the extent of his power. Christ recognized the leadership of Satan, and the unity of his subjects under his control, when he said, "If Satan be divided against himself, how shall his kingdom stand?"

Nor need we generalize away this fact by supposing Satan to be a name for bad spirits in general. The first necessity of a vast society of evil spirits is a leader, a chief around whom they may organize, and through whose one will they may express and enforce their combined power of evil. There may be organized unity in hell as well as in heaven.

Why, then, should men hesitate to admit the existence of a personal devil? The universe is vast; its populations are various and numerous. Bad men exist; why not bad spirits? And if they exist, why may they not exert their malign influence in this world as well as elsewhere?

The various objections to Satan's personal existence may be reduced to this one — the difficulty there is in seeing how a finite being can be every where, and with every body, carrying on his processes of temptation at the same time.

There are several not unreasonable suppositions which may help to remove this difficulty, and dispose of the objections which grow out of it.

It may be that evil spirits are sufficiently numerous to supply each of the inhabitants of our world with such an attendant, or even with a legion of them.

The so-called clairvoyant power may help to illustrate the facility with which spiritual beings are able to read men's thoughts at a great distance. The ability to read them may be a power also to influence them. We know not how great and how varied may be the agency of disembodied spirits.

Satan's power of locomotion may help to account for his seeming omnipresence. Even our vast material sun, with its attendant worlds, is proved by astronomy to rush through space at the rate of fifty-seven miles in a second. If Satan, with his ethereal vehicle, should make no better time than this, he could go round our globe in less than an hour and a quarter. Light travels at the rate of 200,000 miles in a second; and if Satan were able to ride on sunbeams, he would go four times round the earth and back again in a single minute. Shakspeare's imagination was too slow when he allowed one of his ethereal spirits forty minutes to "put a girdle round the earth." Electricity moves still quicker than light; and if there be any thing in the realm of spirits answering to our telegraph, and should Satan prove to be an "operator" there, he can remain at his imperial palace in Pandemonium, and send his dispatches with a terrible rapidity whithersoever and to whomsoever he will.

And again, if, in the realm of spirits, as the poets sing and the philosophers say, wishes are wings, we may dismiss all objection to Satan's existence and influence in the world, founded on the ideas of time and space.

And it may be further said, that the constant presence of Satan with the souls of men may not be necessary to the accomplishment of his purposes. "Going to and fro in the earth, and walking up and down in it," he may lodge some of his seed-lies in a man's mind in early life, and leave them to bring forth their bitter, inevitable fruit. He can give the lie a contagion which will make it catch from mind to mind, as, in a great conflagration, the flames fly from roof to roof till a whole city is in ashes. He can leave the delusion to work on through the organic relations of the family and of society, from generation to generation, with very little subsequent agency of his own.

If it be said that there is "no other devil than man's wicked heart," how then shall we account for the temptations of Christ? Had he a wicked heart to be his tempter?

It is impossible to harmonize the Bible with the denial of Satan's personality. Nor is any thing gained by denying it. To believe a lie has the same ruinous effect, whether the authorship of it is with Satan or ourselves. If Satan were to be regarded as only an impersonation of man's wickedness, so that each man is, after all, his own Beelzebub, his own father of lies, his own tempting, tormenting, and destroying angel, this would not help the matter. It would be no easier to exorcise this self-devil than to escape the influence of a separate, personal tempter. On the other hand, to know that Satan exists, and that he seeks our ruin, is to guard the mind against him; and to know what his lies are, unless we are so wicked as to prefer falsehood to truth, is to dissolve their power over us.

No doubt Satan, considering the end he has in view, would gladly persuade us to ignore his personality, and to account *his* agency as *our own*. This device would enable him to work on unsuspected, and the influence of his lies would not be hindered by his own bad personal reputation.

CHAPTER III.

CHARACTER OF SATAN.

<small>He was a murderer from the beginning, and abode not in the truth, because there is no truth in him. — *John* 8: 44.</small>

SATAN is a moral being, and must have character, good or bad. He is no neuter.

So far as his names are significant, they show him to be wholly wicked. Being the Father of lies, being the Enemy of God and man, surely there can be no virtue in him; he is without a redeeming trait. Although he may retain something of the dignity which belongs to great powers of mind, and may be, by such

"merit, raised
To that bad eminence"

which Milton awards him, yet the Scriptures nowhere represent him as exhibiting any of that natural goodness, that generosity, candor, forbearance, or humanity, which, in mankind, often co-exists with great moral depravity.

Satan has set himself to thwart the will of God against which he has revolted, and devoted all his powers to the execution of his dire purpose. He seeks to subvert men from their allegiance to God, and to lead them captive at his will. He is contending for the moral supremacy of the race. God claims it; Satan has usurped it, and will, to the bitter end, struggle to maintain it. God requires all moral agents to make the well-being of ALL the supreme object of choice and pursuit. This is right and holy; and the divinely secured result is heaven. The doctrine of Satan is, that each moral agent shall make his own individual well-being the object of supreme choice and effort. This is wrong; it is treason against God, and rebellion against the whole order and nature of things; and its fixed result is hell.

The wickedness of Satan appears in the fact, that the great object of the incarnation was "to destroy the works of the devil" (1 John 3: 8), and to liberate man from his bondage (Heb. 2: 4). It is shown by the fact, also, that the apostolic commission was "to turn men from Satan unto God, that they might receive forgiveness of sins" (Acts 26: 15-18). His character is seen, also, in the fact that the saints are solemnly summoned to put on the whole armor of God, that they may successfully wrestle with the devil, and stand against his wiles (Eph. 6: 11-20).

The Bible represents Satan as engaged in all forms of evil, and among all generations of men. He seduced Eve into eating the forbidden fruit. He tempted Cain to kill his brother, and thus made himself "a murderer from the beginning." He persecuted Job in the earliest age of the race. He put it into the heart of David to number the people, and of Judas to betray Christ, and of Ananias to lie unto the Holy Ghost. He did his utmost to foil the Son of God himself.

We see the character of Satan, moreover, in the means he uses to accomplish his ends. Utterly unscrupulous, he puts light for darkness, and darkness for light, and thus confounds the fundamental principles of morals. Infinite Truth is, at his bidding, betrayed to the mob of passions, mocked, scourged, nailed to the cross, and her tomb guarded to prevent resurrection. He attacks the babe in its cradle, and puts lies on infant tongues wherewith to lead them astray from their birth. To play the wolf among the lambs of Christ's flock, is his special delight. He is serpent, wolf, lion, and adder, all in one. He must know full well that the supreme selfishness into which he leads men to plunge themselves, carries in it all crime, all war, all disorder, woe, and ruin; and yet, malignantly and remorselessly, he persists in his course.

Satan's wickedness is all his own, and is as great as he can make it. The greatness of his sin in tempting, does not, however, diminish that of men in yielding to his wicked solicitations. Our adversary can not lead us astray without our own consent.

CHAPTER IV.

THE BATTLE FIELD SURVEYED.—THE HUMAN MIND AND ITS PRINCIPLES OF ACTION.

So God created man in his own image, in the image of God created he him. — *Gen.* 1:27.

If we would be victorious in the warfare to which we are called against the powers of darkness, we can not too well know the field of contest, the human mind, whereon the struggle centers.

As to our mental constitutions, we are "made in the image of God." Our powers are like his in kind, though not in reach. They qualify us "to reason with him" (Isa. 1:18; Ezek. 18:25), to test his truth (1 Thess. 5:21), to understand his will, to know and choose between the right and wrong, to sympathize with and be "like him" in character; in short, to know, love, and obey him, and, in our measure, to live the same moral life which he lives.

The various powers of the mind, like those of the natural universe, sustain important and changeless relations to each other, which need to be understood.

Satan, doubtless, aims to secure the false and wicked action of our minds, both toward God and man. We need, therefore, to survey the ground, and learn where the enemy will wheel his columns, and where he will plant his artillery; how he will shield himself from our weapons; how construct his plots and manage his surprises; and how he will fortify himself, and render his position, if possible, unassailable. We must study the field, also, that we may know where are our own "strongholds," where the "munition of rocks," where the "hiding place from the wind and a covert from the tempest," and where we may make a sure stand against the foe. Other things being equal, the army which best knows the field gains the victory. And we must know the field *before we fight;* the reporters can study and describe it after the battle.

We make no apology for asking here the reader's special attention.

The Mind's Powers.

Of these there are three, a trinity, which are fundamental — a knowing power, a feeling power, an acting power. We know, we feel, we act. We have thought, we have emotion, we have volition. The names of these powers are, the Intellect, the Sensibility, the Will.

Our knowing faculty, the intellect, is a power to know a great variety of things, and with different degrees and kinds of knowledge. Some things we know positively and beyond all doubt, as, for instance, the axioms in mathematics. So we know such moral axioms as these: "every event must have a cause;" "right and wrong are moral opposites," the one deserving praise, the other blame; "virtue ought to be loved and vice hated." The intellect sees the truth of such things directly, without any reasoning, and knows them with a certainty which can not be diminished nor increased.

Other things we know by evidence which comes to us from without; and we know them, confidently or only probably, according to the evidence we gain. Some of the things we know are only the possibilities pictured by the imagination; some are conclusions of the judgment; some are only sensations made upon us by external objects through the senses; some are only reflections awakened by these sensations; some are the records upon the tablets of the memory. The philosophers classify the knowing department of the mind according to these different forms and degrees of knowledge which the intellect gives us.

Through the emotional department of our minds we are the subjects of a great variety of experiences. Innumerable feelings throng the sensibility. In this faculty we may have the rapture of heaven or the rolling sea of hell. Love, joy, purity, and all associated graces here give us their blessing; and here also envy, jealousy, revenge, and kindred passions kindle their lurid flames.

The will is the executive department of our being,

and its capacity is wonderful. We can not will the light into existence, as God did when he said, "Let there be light," but we can will it to shine through our lenses, and engrave our pictures, or reveal to us other worlds innumerable, both above and below the reach of the naked eye. We can not will matter into existence, but we can will it into such forms as we please; we can level the mountains and fill the valleys, and turn the wilderness into a fruitful field. We can not create the forces of the natural world, but we can harness them to our chariots and make them do our bidding. We can not create the distinction between good and evil, right and wrong, but we can will to do the one and to reject the other. We can not swerve the will of God in the least, but we can will our own subordination to it, and so be at one with the Most High.

Some of the Laws of Mind.

1. The intellect is under the law of necessity. When certain conditions are fulfilled, to know is unavoidable. If your open eye is upturned to the unclouded sun, you can not help knowing that it shines. Our agency in gaining knowledge lies in the power which the will has to direct the attention of the knowing faculty. We can use that in whatever way we please.

The agency of the will over the intellect has its

limitations. The knowledge of good and evil is in the mind independently of the will. So of all first truths. The will can not exclude them. Men have their senses open, and the world without teems with thought which it offers to the mind of man; and much knowledge, therefore, enters the intellect without any apparent agency of the will. But all knowledge, so falling in upon the mind involuntarily, as well as that which is gained by the voluntary application of the intellect, and that which inheres in the reason itself, constitutes so much material which the will is free to use for a right purpose or a wrong one. God holds us responsible to use it as the moral law prescribes.

2. The same law of necessity pertains to the sensibility. It has no power of choice in itself. If you put your hand in the flame, the sensation of pain is inevitable. The emotions will correspond to the objects before the mind. It does not follow that the emotions of all persons will be alike in view of the same objects, for there are constitutional differences in this power as well as in other faculties of the mind, and in the bodily senses. Nevertheless, all the control we can have of the sensibility, we have through the will.

3. The law of the will is freedom, not necessity. Not that the will is free in the sense that you can avoid choosing. Choose you must, one way or the other, between good and evil. Life and death are

set before us, and not to choose the one is to take the other. But, between the two, the good and the evil, the right and the wrong, we are, in the very constitution of the will, endowed with the power and liberty of choice. Here is our moral sovereignty; and on this sublime prerogative, which makes us men, all our responsibility hinges.

This freedom we know we have as an essential attribute of our being. The thief who stole your purse knew he could as freely let it alone as take it. Of this he was as conscious as he was of his existence, or of the wickedness of taking it. The freedom of the will, in the sense defined, is known by the highest possible evidence. It is divinely certified to us through our own consciousness. We debate with ourselves whether we shall do this or that, because we know we have the power to choose between them. We hold ourselves and others responsible on the same ground. There ought to be no difference in opinion on this question among men, as there is none in practice.

If it be said that we can not choose in the entire absence of motives, I admit it. Nor are we required to do so. The law of right is in the reason, and life and death are there so set before us, that it is impossible to plead the absence of motive. In a subsequent chapter, we hope to show the truth in the apparently opposite theories of freedom and necessity, and their harmony with each other.

3 *

4. The free will has a law of generic action. One great choice involves many subordinate ones. We form a purpose to build a house, and in this choice there will be a multitude of minor volitions which are required to carry it into execution. A tree has a number of large branches, a greater number of limbs, and a still greater number of leaves; and the life of the tree comes up from the roots, and diffuses itself through, and works in all parts of it. Now, the comprehensive purpose or end for which we have chosen to live, whether it be to please ourselves on the one hand, or God on the other, so far as we have learned to be consistent, will diffuse itself through, and work in all departments of our being, like the life of the tree. The current of that purpose, if it be the one our Savior requires, will carry in it the grace and blessing of God, and every fiber of our moral being will be refreshed and will grow by it, as every part of the tree grows by means of the life current which circulates through it from root to leaf. It will carry the divine life to all the powers of our minds, and set them vibrating in harmony with the will of Heaven. Our characters are as the one great comprehensive choice or end for the accomplishment of which we live; for that infolds all the rest. If your great end be right, and you remain true to that, your life, in all its details, will be well pleasing to God.

5. It is a law of the mind to form its purposes and

to retain them in view of motives or reasons. These are of two general classes — good and evil, right and wrong. We are constituted so as to be able to distinguish between the two. All the reasons there are in the universe in favor of right choice and conduct, and against wrong, are so many motives to us to form and forever retain the right governing choice. All the reasons which God and angels have for rectitude, we have. Three worlds are crowded with the weightiest motives to the right; and not one good reason can be found, in heaven, earth, or hell, for a selfish and sinful life.

6. The mind, by all its laws and powers, is adapted to the right and true. Reason and conscience are on the side of God. The soul's deepest outcry is, "Who will show us any good?" and it refuses to be satisfied till it finds the good which God has provided for it in himself. It is in the mind to approve truth and justice, and to shrink from falsehood and wrong. We are made to appreciate and to be moved by all manifestations of order, beauty, and benevolence, and therefore to be drawn toward God by the exhibitions he is constantly giving to the world of all his perfections. It is not the fault of our constitutions, therefore, if we alienate ourselves from God, and destroy our souls.

7. The relation of the mind's powers to each other is such and so intimate, that the misuse of one inflicts injury upon them all, just as, "when one

member of the body suffers, all the members suffer with it." Pervert the conscience, pollute the sensibility, warp the judgment, and no man can estimate the mischievous consequences, both to the mind and the character.

Conclusion. — The great problem of life must then be this: *How to subordinate the will, and, so, the whole circle of mind-powers under its control, to the will of God, and hold it there against all the opposing influence of Satan and the world.*

"Hic labor, hoc opus est." Can it be done? It can, or the gospel is a lie, and the experience of Paul a delusion. To this end, God works in us and with us. Let us learn the way, let us see how to make use of the gospel as the very "power and wisdom of God" to this end, and the result shall be sure.

CHAPTER V.

WHAT MUST BE SATAN'S METHODS OF WORKING, AS INDICATED BY THE CHANGELESS LAWS OF OUR MENTAL AND MORAL CONSTITUTIONS.

After the working of Satan, with all power and signs and lying wonders.— 2 *Thess.* 2: 9.

AN old student of Mental and Moral Philosophy, Satan doubtless possesses great skill in influencing mind, and warping it into his service. From what has been said in the last chapter, we may learn something of his methods of mischief. For, as we must adapt the machinery we would have driven by steam to the laws of steam, so Satan must fit his measures to the laws of the mind he seeks to control by them.

The ultimate purpose of Satan will, of course, be to gain the control of the will, and to bring it into subjection to his own, instead of the divine will. If he carries that, he is master of the field.

The will acts in view of motives. The leading object of the adversary will be that indicated in 2 Cor. 4 : 3, 4 — to hide Christ, in whose character all right motives are seen in their greatest purity and power, from the mind's view, " lest the light of his glorious gospel should shine " home effectually upon the will, and fix it in its obedience to God. This would be a game of "cutting off supplies" from the soul, of starving the heart by robbing it of that bread which, alone, can satisfy its mighty hunger. It is an attempt to extinguish the soul's sunlight, and drive it back, and hold it in the night of sin — a work well befitting the Prince of Darkness.

The adversary will next ply the mind with falsehood, setting before it lies instead of truth. He will dress them in the garb of truth, and render them as fascinating and persuasive as possible, thus luring men to destruction.

He will, in various ways, seek to secure the adoption of a false general and reigning purpose; one that will not, in truth, answer the demand of Christianity; one that will be just defective enough to ruin the soul, though, to appearance, it may be as fair as that of the men who sat in Moses' seat in the days of Christ. Too much caution can not be exercised here.

A comprehensive and fearfully destructive measure of Satan will be to induce in men a perversion of the judgment and conscience. What vast ruin Satan brought upon the Jews by pushing them into the judgment that Christ was an impostor and a deceiver! Love him, henceforth, they could not; hate him they must. No thought, feeling, or purpose toward him could be otherwise than wrong. Their cry, "Crucify him, crucify him," was the natural sequence of their misjudgment of Christ. And so, universally, the wicked use of this faculty involves the most startling and mischievous consequences. When Saul of Tarsus had perverted his conscience, he could " breathe out threatenings and slaughter" in the name of the Most High !

Again : Satan will make it a strong point to satisfy men with a mere religion of the intellect or the sensibility, that he may thereby retain the control of the will. It would not be possible for him to extinguish the religious nature of man; and probably he does not waste time in such an undertaking. The next thing would be to satisfy this religious nature with something short of God, with a religion of good thoughts, excellent principles, and even of truth *in the letter;* with a religion of good feelings, of warm desires for the crown of glory and the heavenly mansion — a religion which shall just fall short of enthroning God and his truth *in the will.*

Again : Satan will do his utmost to throw the intellect into utter confusion and bewilderment on the whole subject of personal religion. There is no more effectual way to prevent the right action of the mind, than by involving it in such a state. Are not whole masses of men in just this condition? They know not what to believe, which way to turn. They are held in " chains of darkness," groping about in a moral confusion worse than chaos.

Again : as the mind is made for enjoyment, and can not well live without it, Satan may be expected to promise pleasure in his service. He will invest worldliness with all possible charms, and render it as attractive as possible; and on the other hand, will insist that religion is joyless and repulsive. By keeping men pleased with themselves and delighted with their sinful courses, he will retain the control of their wills. In the judgment of some philosophers, if Satan can give the sensibility the impression that the greatest good is to be found in a selfish life, then they can not help sinning. It is certain, by all philosophy, that Satan's strongest hold upon the mind lies in making sin appear as the greatest good — the greatest source of happiness.

CHAPTER VI.

PRIMARY IMPORTANCE TO THE CHRISTIAN LIFE OF THE RIGHT ADJUSTMENT OF THE WILL TO THE TRUTH, ILLUSTRATED BY A "PASTOR'S SKETCH."

Seeing ye have purified your souls in obeying the truth.—1 *Pet.* 1: 22.

THE right working of the will is to the Christian life what the right application of the power is to the movement of the machinery. Since all the other powers of the mind act under the leadership of the will, its subordination to the truth becomes the indispensable condition of all Christian growth and experience. If it be in alliance with ideas which are false, the whole action of the mind must be wrong; and the first thing to be done, cost what it may, is to dissolve that connection, and secure the firm committal of the will to what is true.

We wish here to draw special attention to a mental state — the adjustment of the will to truth or falsehood ; not so much now to the influence of truth or error, as to that state of the mind in which the one or the other becomes operative in the soul for good or evil. For this purpose, it is not material what the false idea which enslaves the will may be, and my object will be well enough served by using, as an illustration, the following " Pastor's Sketch : " —

A gentleman once called upon the writer, during a powerful work of the Spirit, for personal religious conversation. He had never made a profession of religion, nor was he known in the community as entertaining the Christian hope: yet he did secretly cherish the idea that he was a Christian. He was, however, ill at ease in his present state of mind, and wished to know how he might attain a more satisfactory assurance that he was indeed accepted of Christ. From his delineation of his case, it appeared that he found the word precious to his soul; that he was in the habit of retiring alone for prayer, without even allowing his family to know the fact, and that he loved the sanctuary. He had but poorly learned the lessons of faith, and was much in bondage to the fear of man. His will had no such vigorous alliance to the truth as to make it to him the power and wisdom of God for his deliverance. Indeed, it was evidently enslaved to some false ideas which effectually held him in bondage. It was evident that a new adjustment of his voluntary powers was demanded, or his progress in the divine life was out of the question. Foreseeing the difficulty of dislodging the adversary and bringing his mind under Christ's sway, I resorted to the following method: I said to him, "I think I can make a suggestion which you would do well to follow." "And what is it?" he asked. "I can not tell you until you pledge yourself to do what I shall recommend." "But I dare not promise till I know what it is." "Why not? Can you not trust me that it will be all right? You have had confidence to come to me for advice. I am a minister of Christ, I hope, and shall only ask you to do what I most fully believe he would have you do." "But perhaps I can not do it." "And do you think I would ask you to do what you can not do? God forbid." "But it may not be proper for me to do it." "Would you, then, impeach my character by assuming that I would ask you, in the name of Christ, to do an improper thing?" "O, no, sir, I would not." "If, moreover, your conscience shall honestly forbid your doing what I shall propose, I will not then ask you to do it, nor even consent to your doing it." "Will you not tell me unless I promise?" "I can not; it would not be best; I want you should trust me. You do not expect to know all the will of God before you pledge him universal obedience: you *trust him* that his requirements will be right. I want you should trust me on the same principle." "Well, I will try to do it." "No, that is not what I want. Deciding to try to do a thing is often very different from deciding *to do it*. If I should ask you to lift a weight of three thousand pounds, you might well say you would try, through a suspicion that you could not lift it; but if I ask you to lift a weight of ten pounds, your decision would not be to *try*, but *to do it*. God requires us to decide to obey him; and if we merely decide to try to obey him, we shall only make a self-righteous use of our powers, and fail. Now, when you will decide to do the proposed thing, I will tell you." "You will not ask me to do a hard thing?" O, no; a very simple thing; I do it every day, and have great pleasure in it." "*Well, well, I will do it.*" "Very well. What I propose is, that, this night, you erect a family altar in your house, and call your household about it, and with them worship God." "O, sir, I can not do that; I am sure I can not." "Certainly you can do it; I know you can." "It is right, I know. I have often felt the duty pressing heavily upon me, but I have as often sunk down under the conscious conviction that it was impossible for me to do it." "Now, let me show you your difficulty: your *will* is *committed* to the idea that you can not do it, and this binds your mind, and is the whole secret of your failure. But that idea is false; it is a lie of the Devil. The *truth* is, you *can* pray in your family as well as elsewhere. You tongue will serve you there; God will help you even more certainly at the family altar than elsewhere, for he loves to be honored there." "I wish I could do it." "You can, if you will drop the lie, and let your will adjust itself to what is true, and cling to that." "But I *feel* as if I could not possibly do it." "I know you feel so, but it is because you are holding a lie in your intellect, and that determines the feeling; cast out the falsehood, and take hold of the truth, and you will not fail." At length the lie was wrested from its dominion over the will, and the truth took its place. The remainder of the day was delightfully spent, in the quiet confidence that he had substantially secured the victory, which would be completely achieved in the evening. Returning from meeting that night, as he was entering his yard, his joys forsook him, and his soul seemed overwhelmed in darkness; and then the feeling that he could not erect that altar pressed him to the earth. But he remembered his promise, and the instruction he had received. He called the promises of God to his aid. He remembered that He was personally near who had said, "My grace is sufficient for thee," who had bidden a man stretch forth his withered arm; and, although his depression was terrible, he insisted that he could and would fulfill his vow. He called his family together, and established his altar. The spell was broken; the lie was now effectually dethroned, and the truth brought him victory. He could pray in his family as easily as in his closet.

The principle is universal. If the will be adjusted to falsehood, the whole mind is so far enslaved and corrupted; if to truth, all the powers work in liberty and righteousness. The gospel of Christ is indeed the power and wisdom of God unto salvation, but only when the will, by the grace of God, is properly adjusted to it. The most essential and fundamental of all conditions of salvation is, therefore, that the will, by faith, grasp the truth in Christ, and Christ in the truth, — for he is "the way, the truth, and the life," — and hold it fast, even unto the death. For the want of this proper adjustment, the whole gospel, including the promises of Christ and the ministry of the spirit, is rendered completely inoperative. Thousands in our churches have committed their wills to the idea that they can not pray in their families; and the very altar which stands nearest to God is banished from their dwellings, and innumerable households sit in darkness. By the same sort of misadjustment, multitudes are kept from confessing Christ; and a large number in our churches are utterly powerless for any spiritual and effective service in the great work of salvation. The helm of their being is in the hands of the foe. All divine help is lost to the soul because the mental machinery — so to speak — is not properly connected with the great wheel of God's truth, in whose ceaseless rotations lies the power by which alone salvation is given to the world.

The intellect may be so adjusted to the truth that a man may be perfectly orthodox in sentiment; the sensibility may be so related to the truth, that the prophet of God shall be to the soul "as a very lovely song of one that hath a pleasant voice, and can play well on an instrument," yet if the will be not linked to the word of life, *all is lost*. This, Satan understands full well, and acts accordingly.

All the dishonesty, deceit, covetousness, party

spirit, and whatever else of sin and selfishness there is in the church and world, results simply from the voluntary alliance of men's wills with false and conflicting ideas. For the same reason, men find the exercise of the benevolence which Christ requires a distasteful duty rather than a blessed luxury, and the performance of religious services both unwelcome and unsatisfying.

To introduce the millennium, and fill the world with the peace of God, it is only necessary that this ruinous allegiance should be broken up, and that the wills of men should be indissolubly linked to the simple truth as it is in Jesus Christ. And all the sweet influences which flow down from the heart of the Father, and all the healing mercies which radiate from the throne of the heavenly grace, and which are borne to the very door of our inner being by the Eternal Spirit, are designed to secure and cement this glorious union of the soul to Him who is the source of all life and glory to fallen man. Only as this result is attained can we be such Christians as our own happiness, the age in which we live, and the Bible demand we should be. It is one of the unaccountable mysteries of sin, that the human heart should rebel against such a heavenly and blessed consummation.

CHAPTER VII.

SATAN THE "AUTHOR AND FINISHER" OF UNBELIEF.

Take heed, brethren, lest there be in any of you an evil heart of unbelief, in departing from the living God. — *Heb.* 3 : 12.

The Scriptures teach that salvation is by faith alone. "He that believeth shall be saved." "He that believeth not shall be damned." "Whatsoever is not of faith is sin." "This is the work of God, that ye believe on Him whom he hath sent." Christ is the "author and finisher of faith;" the adversary, in a similar sense, doubtless, is the inspirer of unbelief. In order to understand Satan's power of evil in this capacity, we need a distinct conception of what are the elements of faith and unbelief.

Faith, then, implies an object. Without this, there is nothing on which the mind can repose its confidence, and faith will be naturally impossible. This object must be revealed to the mind, the intellect must see it, or faith can not be. To trust in a person of whom you have no knowledge is impossible. Nor would it help me to trust *in you*, reader, to have some one else bear testimony to me concerning you. Do you say that, "on the testimony of A, whom I know, to the reliability of B, I trust my life in the keeping of the latter?" But your trust is really in A, not in B, although you have put yourself in his hands. Suppose, before B is personally known to you, you find that you have entirely misunderstood A, who meant to assure you that B was wholly untrustworthy. You would then see that your confidence rested in A, and not in B. Your trust must repose in the witness alone, until the third party becomes personally known to you: then it can pass over and rest in him, if he be found worthy.

Again: the object of faith so presented to the mind *must be closed in with by the will.* To see the truth and enthrone it as the law of our voluntary being, is to believe unto life. To see the truth, approve it with the reason, and to refuse, by the soul's voluntary act or state, to enthrone it as our law of life and conduct, is to be guilty of fatal unbelief. The voluntary element, or the want of it, in our faith, makes all the difference between a living and a dead faith — between a religion of forms and one of life and power. To see the truth on which our faith must repose in order to salvation, is not virtue; but, seeing it, to will it. The devils see it, and, rebelling against it, tremble in their guilt before its majesty. To see the truth does not save. To see it is condemnation; but seeing it, and welcoming it to perfect lordship over us, is to unite the soul to its Redeemer, and make it a joyful partaker of his life.

Man, by sin, has lost his confidence in God — not the sentiment that God is worthy of confidence, not the knowledge of his truth absolutely and entirely, for the law is engraven on the reason — but that living faith, the essential element of which, after the truth is seen, consists in its enthronement in the will, as the all-governing law of life and duty.

Now, the office of Christ as the author and finisher of faith is, by all divine moral influences, to bring men to that vital enthronement of the truth in the will and heart, which must be secured in order to the possibility of salvation. He is the Logos, the Word, the Revealer of God to men. By his manifestation of the divine object of faith, trust in God becomes possible. Our coöperating act, not merely of seeing, but of crowning the truth and its Lord, as supreme in the soul, completes the exercise of saving faith, and puts us in the kingdom.

On the other hand, Satan becomes the author and finisher of unbelief, by hiding from the mind the true object of saving faith, and thus he renders its exercise impossible. When the truth reaches the intellect, he will obscure, pervert, and distort it, and bring all possible influences within his reach to bear upon the mind to prevent the will from so closing in with it as is indispensable to a vital and saving faith. "But if our gospel be hid, it is hid to them that are lost; in whom the god of this world hath blinded the minds of them which believe not, lest the light of the glorious gospel of Christ, who is the image of God, should shine unto them" (2 Cor. 4 : 3, 4). This touch of an apostolic pen gives us Satan's method of counteracting the work of Christ as the inspirer of faith, and of holding the will in its state of ruinous unbelief.

Through the exercise of faith, as here defined, the whole gospel becomes operative in the soul for its salvation.

CHAPTER VIII.

SATAN, IN THE HEIGHT OF HIS POWER, OBSCURING THE ESSENTIAL OBJECT OF FAITH, CHRIST JESUS THE LORD; THUS RENDERING IMPOSSIBLE THE EXERCISE OF A LIVING FAITH.

In whom the god of this world hath blinded the minds of them which believe not, lest the light of the glorious gospel of Christ, who is the image of God, should shine unto them.—2 *Cor.* 4:4.

SATAN'S victory is to hold the mind in unbelief. He wins the battle if he can succeed in hiding from our interior view faith's proper object, which is God in Christ, who alone can forgive sin and bestow the gift of eternal life.

We have already shown that the object of faith must be made known to the mind, in order to the exercise of a living trust on our part.

Let us advance a step, and show that God alone can make this indispensable manifestation of himself to us. Mind is sovereign in the realm of its own personality; it is self-revealing; one person can not manifest the personality, the inner life, of another; much less can a finite reveal the Infinite Spirit. We may learn something *about* God from his works, and from our natures, which he has stamped with his own likeness; but in order to a new-creating faith, and the divine life in us, God must manifest *himself*— himself as distinct from all other beings — to our interior consciousness. This truth is reflected in, and illustrated by our human relations. It is when two individuals fully and mutually reveal *themselves* to each other, each inviting the other to repose in him an unlimited and generous confidence, each giving himself to the other in a unity of love, that there springs up a life of joyous and blessed experiences, which otherwise would have been naturally impossible. So it is, when God personally manifests himself to us, and takes our willing spirits into all loving and confidential relations to himself, and allows us to behold what we are able of his glory, that there springs up within us a new life indeed, the very life of God, of which sin had deprived us, and we are saved.

On all sides it is agreed that the mission of Christ was to give to the world this needed divine manifestation. He was, therefore, "God manifest in the flesh" — the object of saving faith. God he must have been himself, or he could not have manifested him to the world in a way to restore the life lost by sin.

Our Unitarian friends, who deny the Deity of Christ, insist that he can yet reveal to us more about God than we are able to comprehend; and, therefore, that his Deity is in no way essential to his mission as our Savior. But their fallacy lies in the assumption that to know something *about* God is equivalent to knowing God *himself* by his own personal manifestation, which surely is not true. God, as personally and lovingly manifested to the soul, is the object on which our faith must fix itself, not something concerning him which some other, some finite being may report to us. The wickedest men may learn all that is knowable *about* God by his works and by the testimony of others; and yet, lacking his own manifestation, they will remain dead in trespasses and sins.

Logically, therefore, it will be the masterpiece of Satanic skill to hide from the world the Deity of Christ, that he may thus remove from men the pillar of fire and cloud, and leave them to wander in the dark wilderness of unbelief.

Consider how effectually he has wrought in this high place of his power. There are whole denominations of professed Christians who systematically deny his Deity. They come with Philip to Christ, and say, "Lord, show us the Father, and it sufficeth us;" and then fail to apprehend the deep significance of those reproving and yet life-giving words of Christ in reply: "*Have I been so long time with you, and yet hast thou not known me, Philip? He that hath seen me hath seen the Father; and how sayest thou, then, Show us the Father?*" Thus was Philip rebuked for looking after God as the object of faith and love elsewhere than in Christ.

Scarcely less successful has he been with multitudes who theoretically hold to the Deity of Christ. Their practical unbelief obscures his divine attributes. It locates him eighteen hundred years in the distant past, and they know him not as an ever-present, Almighty Deliverer. This eclipse of the Sun of Righteousness enshrouds the whole matter and method of their salvation in darkness.

It is difficult to see how Satan should so obscure the Deity of Christ from men who have the Bible and profess to believe it. It is true he was called the *Son* of God; but that title was given him simply as having been divinely begotten in the flesh (Luke 1 : 35). He was not known as the Son of God in his pre-existent state, and the question is, Who was he then? Even if he were but the Son of God, we ought to conclude that, in nature and attributes, he was the equal of his Father; for all sons, so far as we know, are so equal to their fathers. Nor does it seem good reasoning to conclude that, if there are three persons in the Godhead, there must be three Gods. There does not appear to be any more absurdity in the supposition that the one omnipresent, essential Spirit should manifest himself by a threefold personality, in some respects different from each other, than that the one limited, essential spirit, man, should manifest himself through a threefold set of attributes, each in important respects different from the others, and each having its own department of the body, — the intellect having the brain, the sensibility, the nerves of sensation, and the will, the muscular system, — wherewith to perform its assigned functions. The one fact is no more absurd, scarcely more incomprehensible, than the other.

Opening our Bibles, the Supreme Being who stands out on its pages is plainly the Lord Jesus Christ. That God, who " in the beginning made the heavens and the earth," the New Testament abundantly shows to have been Christ. The creative volition was his, even though he issued it under the direction of the Father; and the heavens must be regarded as testifying to the "eternal power and Godhead" of Christ, their Maker (Rom. 1 : 20).

Again : farther down the line of revelation, some Being appears to Moses in the burning bush, who reveals himself as the I AM THAT I AM, the God of the fathers, Abraham, Isaac, and Jacob; who makes himself known by his hitherto undisclosed and more sacred name JEHOVAH, which he thrice repeats. If the self-existent God of the universe reveals himself any where in the Bible, it is here. The burning bush becomes the pillar of cloud and fire, and from this Shechinah, this same Being leads the people through the wilderness. But who was this Being? We have only to read Paul's sketch of this journey of the Israelites (1 Cor. 10), and his statement (Heb. 11 : 26), that Moses esteemed the reproach of CHRIST greater riches than the treasures of Egypt, to learn that, in his judgment, it was Christ who revealed himself to Moses, and therefore, that the self-existent Jehovah of the Old Testament, and the pre-existent Christ of the New, were identically the same Being.

Again: still later in the Bible, we find nearly a score of passages in which the one Supreme Being insists upon his unity in the most positive terms, declaring that "there is no God beside" him; "he is God, and there is none else;" "he is God in heaven above and upon the earth beneath: there is none else." And yet this one only God characterizes himself in such a way as absolutely to identify him as no other than the pre-existent Messiah. He declares that he is "the King of Israel," and his "Redeemer;" he is "the first and the last;" he is the God "unto whom every knee shall bow and every tongue swear," and besides whom "there is no Savior;" he is the Jehovah who "made the earth, and created man upon it; who stretched out the heavens, and commanded all their host;" he it was who chose the fathers, and "brought their seed out of Egypt with his mighty power," and made them hear his "voice out of the midst of the fire." Christ, then, is the one God of the Bible. The Father and Spirit are not other Gods, but only separate manifestations of the same God.

And yet Satan blinds the minds of men to the Deity of Christ, and holds them in unbelief. His object is plain. Our salvation demands an Almighty

Savior. If Moses needed assurance from the I Am in order to stand before the throne of Pharaoh, much more do we need it in order to overcome the foes of our salvation. No finite being in our pillar of cloud and fire can lead us through the sea and the wilderness to our Promised Land.

CHAPTER IX.

SATAN'S SECOND ECLIPSE OF THE OBJECT OF FAITH — HIDING ALSO THE DEITY OF THE SPIRIT, AND FOR A LIKE PURPOSE.

Even so the things of God knoweth no man, but the Spirit of God.—
1 *Cor.* 2 : 11.

WHEN Christ, as "God manifest in the flesh," left the world, it was with the promise that he would send the Comforter, whose ministrations would be of more value to the disciples than his longer presence could be (John 16 : 7). While our Lord remained in the body, his Deity was unavoidably vailed by his flesh. His humanity was, of course, specially visible, and made its needed impression. On the human side of the Messiah, the disciples had become familiar with him, and had learned to approach him with confidence. Through the vail, they saw something of his Divinity, something of the "glory which he had with the Father before the world was." But the time had come when they needed to know him more perfectly as to his Divine nature. Their then knowledge left them too weak to stand in the hour of temptation. It was, therefore, "expedient" for Christ to withdraw from the flesh, that their attention might be concentrated upon his Deity.

The Spirit would succeed him, and "take of the things of Christ, and show them unto them." It was not the human side of the Redeemer's being which the Spirit was chiefly to manifest, since, for such a manifestation, it could not have been expedient for Christ to leave the flesh and the human conditions amid which he had shown himself, but rather his eternal power and Godhead, which had been, thus far, so thickly vailed by the flesh. The disciples must know their beloved Leader as very God, or they can not cope with the hostile powers of earth and hell which they are soon to meet. On the day of Pentecost, the Spirit came, and they received a knowledge of their Redeemer which changed their weakness into a courage and power fitting them to revolutionize the world. Henceforward they stood in the fully apprehended Deity of Christ, and spoke with the "tongue of fire"; and, with "Emanuel" on their banner, their course was thenceforward onward and triumphant.

By a logical necessity, then, the Holy Spirit must be God. According to principles already stated, no being but God himself could reveal God. In the performance of his mission, the Spirit did disclose and show to the inner life of the disciples the supreme Divinity of their Master, and, consequently, the infinite value of his words. His mission had a higher significance, simply because he could make that exhibition more clearly and powerfully to the mind than Christ could possibly do it through the vail of his flesh. And it is this which makes the dispensation of the Spirit "excel in glory" all others. By the Spirit's manifestation, we look through all vails, all types and shadows, and behold the glorious reality of God's character and love, and know our God as the life, the joy, and the infinite portion of our souls forever.

The disciples evidently had no other idea than that the Spirit was God. If Ananias "lied to the Holy Ghost," it was against God he lied. To be "born of God" and to be "born of the Spirit" were the same thing. They were all "taught of God," and yet the Holy Ghost was their teacher. Christians are the "temple of God," and yet the God who dwells in them as his temple is the Holy Ghost. Christ, as to his flesh, is the Son of God, of the Highest, and yet he is begotten by the Holy Ghost. Did God inspire the prophets? They "spake as they were moved by the Holy Ghost." Is it God's work to "convince men of sin"? It is the office-work of the Holy Spirit. Is the world in rebellion against God? It is the Holy Spirit they have resisted. Is there one offense against God which is unpardonable? It is the "blasphemy of the Holy Ghost." Is God omnipresent? None can fly from the presence of the Spirit. Is God omniscient? "The Spirit knoweth all things, even the deep things of God." Must men be consecrated to God in order to be saved?

They must be baptized "into the name of the Father, and of the Son, and of the Holy Ghost."

The personality of the Spirit is as clearly recognized in the Scriptures as that of the Father or of Christ.

How obviously, now, it falls in with the purpose of Satan, in holding men in unbelief, to hide from them the personality and Deity of the Spirit, by whom alone the object of saving faith can be effectually manifested! In this way, he obscures the glory, and essentially sets aside the power of the New Testament, which obviously lies in the agency and peculiar ministry of the Spirit; he robs the believer of the great characteristic promise of the Christian Dispensation, distinctly and impressively given by our Lord to his disciples at the closing and most memorable hour of his ministry, that the Holy Spirit should come and abide with them forever, as their Comforter, Teacher, and Sanctifier; he takes away all that which renders the gospel practically better than the law, the substance, than the shadow; he captures the believer's "strongholds," and leaves him without the saving knowledge of the Deliverer.

There are denominations of Christians by whom the personality and Deity of the Spirit are systematically denied. They see in the Spirit no infinite, intelligent Being, mighty to save by his own self-revealing power, but only an impersonal, indefinable *influence*. If men's hearts were not sometimes clearer than their heads, we see not how such could escape the death of unbelief. Nor does an orthodox theory always suffice to save men from the effects of this second eclipse of the object of saving faith.

When the disciple finds God manifested by the Spirit, the difficulties in regard to the Divine mode of existence strangely pass away. Although he may not be able to solve the mystery of the Trinity, he finds the wants of his soul wondrously met as he communes with God, his Father, with the same God, his Redeemer, and with the same God, his Sanctifier. He welcomes to his heart the "Angel of the Covenant," the Messiah whom the Father has sent; and it does not occur to him, that Christ must be less than God in his nature and attributes, because the Father appointed him his "messenger" to a lost world.

CHAPTER X.

THE MISCHIEFS SATAN ACCOMPLISHES BY REMOVING FROM BEFORE THE EYE OF FAITH THE GODHEAD OF CHRIST AND THE SPIRIT.

But if our gospel be hid, it is hid to them that are lost.—2 *Cor.* 4 : 3.

IN the first place, the essential object of saving faith being hidden from the mind, a living trust therein is rendered impossible. We can not rely upon one for any thing beyond what he is able to do with the powers we ascribe to him. If our " God manifest in the flesh," in whom we trust, is only a finite being, we have only a finite Savior, who can not restore to us the " life of God " which is lost by sin. Failing to find Jehovah manifested in Christ, we do not find him at all, and are left to wander in the wilderness of error and unbelief, and, perchance, betake ourselves to a cold naturalism, and grope about to find him in his works. Stars and flowers take the place of the Divine Christ; religious sentimentality and the " works of the flesh " are substituted for the new birth, and men have a "name to live " while yet dead in sin.

Again : another consequence of hiding the Deity of Christ and the Spirit will be, that, although the intellect may, in some sense, apprehend the truth, yet the will, choosing the darkness involved in the pursuit of its own selfish ends, will reject and refuse to obey it until its unbelief does violence to all reason, and to all the sane practice of men on other subjects, and becomes a "marvel" to the Son of God himself. The will does not surrender the weapons of its rebellion except to its Creator and Lord.

Again: in proportion as the true object of faith is hidden by Satan from the mind, the blessings of faith are lost. It is blessed to have faith in any being who is worthy of confidence, and the riches of the experience of faith will correspond to the perceived excellence, the benevolence, and the ability of that being. The promises of God pledge to believers eternal and exhaustless good, as great as their natures will enable them to receive. They are all "yea and amen in Christ," and can bring in them to us no more of Divinity than we apprehend in him. With the eye of our faith open upon *God* revealed to us in Jesus, we dwell in that light which can come only from the Divine Mind; with our hearts stayed *on Him*, "the *peace of God* which passeth all understanding, keeps our hearts and minds through Christ Jesus;" anchoring our being *to Him* by faith, we outride all the storms of earth, and are nearest heaven when on the crest of the topmost wave; with our ear open *to Him*, his word is a sword which cleaves down every foe, or a fountain whose living waters well up and lave and refresh our whole being, and cool the fever of sin; walking *with Him*, we are in "ways of pleasantness and paths of peace;" sitting at *His feet*, our pride is consumed by the glory of his meekness and lowliness of mind; seeing in our duty *His will*, it is the very elixir of privilege to do it; casting the burden of our sins upon *His mercy*, they are gone forever. But, alas! if our faith does not find *Him* manifested, all this is lost; the frosts of sin are not dissolved, and the vibrations of heavenly joy can not reach our hearts.

Again: by hiding the Deity of Christ and the Spirit, Satan shuts the mind up *to its own idea of God as conceived in the darkness of sin*, and deprives it of the right idea *as God himself manifests it*, to inspire a true worship. The result is seen, the world over, in the chaos of false and spurious religions. Every man becomes a god unto himself. The "gods many and lords many," thus conceived, are as antagonistic as selfish men, and as little in harmony as the congress of deities on Olympus. . The social and religious principles becoming allied, men are drawn together in brotherhoods of selfishness, into hierarchies, sects, and warring parties; but their synagogues will be, so far, the "synagogues of Satan." The Satanic graces of pride, jealousy, hatred, revenge, and their like, will combine in a common opposition to that Christianity which derives its life from the Deity of the despised Nazarene, and from that cross to which the same opposition nailed the Son of God.

The idea of God, thus conceived, has no redeeming power in it, but the very opposite. The Pharisees were zealously religious under the idea of God as they found it in their own selfish hearts; Paul, under the idea, as God the Holy Spirit manifested it to him. Their hearts remained as unchanged, and as full of pride and hatred, as his had been before the Divine manifestation met him on his way to Damascus. As they conceived the character of God, they felt it their duty to crucify Christ. As he learned it from God himself, his love for Christ at once became a passion, and he would henceforth glory in nothing but in "Christ and him crucified."

By this process, then, Satan inveigles the mind into all manner of unbelief, and easily leads it captive at his will.

CHAPTER XI.

SATAN SOWING TARES. — PASTOR'S SKETCH ILLUSTRATING THE NECESSITY OF HAVING THE RIGHT SEED-TRUTH SOWN IN THE HEART, THAT A TRUE CHRISTIAN CHARACTER MAY GROW THEREFROM.

The enemy that sowed them is the devil. — *Matt.* 13 : 39.

WHEN Christ charges Satan with sowing tares (Matt. 13 : 25–39), we suppose he means to say that that wicked one disseminates, in the minds of men, ideas and principles, the effect of which will be to counteract the growth and influence of the truth implanted by God himself.

In a large garden, may be found a great variety of plants, differing in their forms, colors, fragrance, and in many of their habits of life. Side by side, they grow from the same soil; the same sun gives them light, the same dews and showers refresh them, and the same hands cultivate them. Whence, then, their differences? They are to be found *in the differing seeds*.

The seeds of character are ideas and purposes planted in the mind. Men grow to be what they are, in all their radical diversities of character, from certain seed-ideas. Let a youth, just budding into manhood, take up the problem of his life. The future is all before him. What shall he do with the powers which are already stirring within him, and which must be exercised? At what shall he aim — at political eminence, at literary distinction, or wealth, or, peradventure, the Christian life? He is absorbed, and his brain aches with the subject. He ponders it long and anxiously, and finally decides, *I will be rich.*

That idea, thus implanted, is the seed of his character now to be unfolded. It germinates in his intellect, and his whole thinking force is applied to the question, How shall I gain wealth? — by what means, on land or sea, by what business, by what principles? It expands in his sensibility, and the entire current of his emotions swells and surges along the channel, of earthly gain. He loves every thing which will give him wealth. The " price current " is his bible. In the strong speech of Carlyle, " to gain is heaven, to lose is hell." The same seed matures in his will; and this mighty central force of the mind works all possible agencies within its reach for the one end of amassing the chosen treasure. This young man thus becomes an apostle Paul *in the opposite direction.*

The seed-idea of Paul's character was this: " Christ and him crucified," all and in all; absolute stewardship to Jesus; all things done in his name and for his glory; Paul, the " old man," dead, and Christ, the "new man," alive in him. From this idea grew the character of the apostle. It completely mastered his intellect so that he would only know Christ and the Cross. It possessed his sensibility so that he rejoiced in tribulation, and wept over lost men, and loved them the more, the less they loved him. It wrought with such living power in his will and heart, that his words, from the moment they were uttered to this day, have been among the most potent moral forces the world has ever felt.

A leading and subtle device of Satan, as an effectual means of inflicting fatal moral injury, is to get an imperfect or incomplete seed-idea planted in the minds of Christian men. As an illustration of the importance of receiving the "good seed" instead of "tares," I present the following: —

Pastor's Sketch.

An excellent parishioner once gave me the following account of his experience, and wished I would point out the difficulty under which he was laboring. He wished to live every day as a Christian should live. His habit was to enter his closet before going to his business in the morning, and not to leave it till he felt that his sins were forgiven, and the smile of his Savior rested on his soul. He then went to his office to transact the business of the day. He soon found himself drifting from the sweet peace with which he left his closet. He was in a different atmosphere. God did not seem near. Temptation would sour and vex his spirit, and easily gain the mastery. In his bargains, he found that he loved himself much better than his customers. It was not easy for him *there* to bear witness for Christ. The glowing heart, with which he left the closet, became hardened and insensible; and at night he found himself far away from Jesus, with his harp unstrung upon the willows. It required bitter repentings, and often many tears, to get back to the place from which he had fallen away. He had gone through the process till his soul was weary, and he longed to find a way of retaining his morning blessing through the day; and, hence, his inquiries.

My reply to his difficulty was on this wise: Your radical idea of the Christian life is incomplete—too narrow. You do not make it include your business. That is *your own*, not *the Lord's*. You leave your Savior in the closet, and go to your office, the servant of A. H. D. Paul's idea of that life was Christ, all and in all, self dead, and Christ living in him. He made tents for the Savior, as truly as he made sermons. There was no division of himself between Christ and Mammon. Yours, on the other hand, is Christ in the closet, and self in the counting-room; Christ in your worship, and self in your business. You have broken in two the very seed-idea of the Christian life, and thrown away an essential part of it. That which you cultivate in your closet does as well as any half-seed can. You must take Paul's root-idea if you would have complete fruit in your experience. *You* need to fail in your business, and make a full assignment at once to Christ, and take your position in the business, not as a principal in the firm, but as the "steward," the "confidential clerk" of your Lord and Master. Then you will find Christ in *his* counting-room as well as in the closet, and *his* business shall no longer be a snare to you, but a means of grace.

His eyes were opened; he made the proposed assignment, and found a blessing richer, every way, than his pastor predicted. The Master was with him all the day; his counting-room was a Bethel; the Divine Presence kept his soul loyal and true; his tongue was loosed; he could sell goods and preach Christ at the same time; and, as he remarked, he "was not tempted to cheat any more in selling leather," for his new Employer did not allow it. At night, he returned to his closet in advance of his morning position, and onward he went, day by day, growing in grace, and in favor with God and with man. Such were the fruits of the true seed fully received into the soul.

It makes all difference, then, in the life of a Christian, whether or not he has the true seed-idea at bottom. Paul had it; and he found the grace of God all-abounding, the power of temptation broken, and the service of Christ his highest delight. His experience was a combination of the greatest possible moral forces, such as hope, love, joy, justice, patience, meekness, and the like, and carried with it, therefore, a living demonstration of the truth of the gospel. But with an essentially defective seed-idea, the religious life must be correspondingly defective and powerless. The whole character is a failure, exhibiting to the world a sad combination of the elements of weakness, sorrow, sighing, doubt, fear, injustice, impatience, and unbelief, repelling other minds from Christ, rather than drawing them sweetly to embrace him.

Thus the "enemy" scatters broadcast over the "field of the world" his tares. What they are, and how they bear their noxious fruit, will appear as we progress.

CHAPTER XII.

SATAN AS THE FATHER OF LIES.—PRINCIPLES PREMISED.

When he speaketh a lie, he speaketh of his own: for he is a liar, and the father of it.— John 8 : 44.

THE tares which Satan sows are the lies which he impresses upon the minds of men. Before exposing some of these falsehoods, we will state several important principles, which need to be considered in this connection.

1. The object of Satan in the use of lies is, of course, to destroy the soul, to confirm it in the darkness, guilt, and ruin of sin.

2. When men accept what are really the lies of Satan, they hold them *as truths;* and the consequence is, that they have all the binding force of truth, and all the damaging effect of lies. The mind is not made for falsehood. It first calls it truth, and then welcomes it to its fatal and ruinous work.

3. While lies have possession of the mind, they, of course, exclude from it the corresponding truths. There is a natural self-consistency in our mental operations. We do not consciously believe that a thing is both true and false at the same time. To

hold as a truth that two and two are six, is to hold as a lie that two and two are four. Some great lie, which the mind may adopt as a truth, will inevitably exclude the whole gospel from the soul as a saving power. If a man holds that he is not a sinner in the Bible sense, the whole gospel becomes a nullity, and can have no significance to him.

4. To believe the lies of Satan against God, involves an impeachment of the Divine character for veracity. It is to transfer the character of Satan to God, and that of God to Satan. It is to account and treat God, "who can not lie," as a liar; and Satan, who is the father of liars, and who will not use the truth except in a way to have the effect of lies, as worthy of all confidence. It is, in our conduct, to undeify Jehovah as to his most essential moral attribute; and this is the very climax of guilt. Nor is it any valid excuse for treating God as a liar by our unbelief, that the promises, in which we refuse to trust, seem "too good" to belong to persons so unworthy as ourselves.

5. The lies of Satan are mainly anchored in the sensibility. The attack of the enemy is not direct upon the reason, for that affirms, intuitively, the existence and veracity of God. Nor is the onset direct upon the will. Satan does not come and nakedly urge a man to set up his will against his Maker and Benefactor, against truth and obligation. He is too wise to fly so palpably in the face of man's

moral nature. He rather plants his lie, sows his tares, in the emotional nature. You *feel* that the thing is true, though reason may say it is false. The *feeling* possesses and haunts you, and you can not rid yourself of it, that, for example, there is no mercy for you; and *feeling* thus, you allow your reason to be silenced, and your *will* to go over to the *feeling*, and *accept* the lie as truth, and Satan's object is accomplished. He has hooked his chain into your will through the lie he planted in your sensibility, and he thus easily leads you "captive at his will." This he will continue to do so long as you will consent to take as true his impressions, instead of the voice of your reason and the positive testimonies of God's word. The whole coast here is lined with wrecks.

6. Satan adapts his lies, varies, changes, multiplies and divides them, to meet the idiosyncrasies, prejudices, and the surroundings of each individual soul whose destruction he seeks. All his skill and knowledge and power of deception, are doubtless employed to turn light into darkness and darkness into light. Fortunately for the world, however, Satan can not succeed in extinguishing the Sun of Righteousness.

7. That Satan has neither tongue nor voice, does not prevent his ministration of lies. Language is one medium of thought in the world, but there is no proof that this is at all necessary in the realm of

spirit. For aught we know, Satan has the same power, in kind, to impress men with falsehood, that the Holy Spirit has to seal truth upon the mind.

8. When lies become thoroughly enthroned in the will, it is very difficult, and often impossible, to dislodge them. They have possession of all the mind's powers, so that every avenue is jealously guarded against the approach of the truth. The whole force of mental habit and of apparent interest, is on the side of falsehood. The power of the mind itself to find and hold the truth is, by the perversion of its faculties, sadly impaired. The difficulty of casting out devils is only the difficulty of casting out lies. No voice but that of the Almighty can effectually command them.

CHAPTER XIII.

THE LIES WHEREBY SATAN KEEPS MEN FROM BECOMING CHRISTIANS.

Why hath Satan filled thine heart, to lie to the Holy Ghost? — *Acts* 5 : 3.

THE falsehoods which Satan impresses upon men are of two classes. By those of one class, he aims to keep them from becoming Christians at all; by those of the other, to prevent Christians from living a true, earnest, and effective life. In the present chapter, we will consider some of the lies of the first class.

Lie No. 1.

We name, first, the original falsehood, which, with serpent tongue, Satan told to Eve — "*Ye shall not surely die.*" In other words, "*No serious consequences are to be apprehended from sin and transgression. The fruit is good; your eyes will be opened; you will become wise. Go on in disregard of God; trample on his law and authority; set up your own will, and live for your own pleasure supremely, and all will be well at last — ye shall not surely die.*"

This, for substance, is the terrible lie. The

masses of mankind, hearing it in alluring tones, lay the flattering unction to their souls. They commit and adjust their wills to it as truth, and thus believe and convert the lie into a seeming reality. They are then prepared to cling to the falsehood, notwithstanding the remonstrances of reason, and the teaching of all analogy and revelation. They live on, transgressing the law of God continually and without a blush.

While the mind clings to this falsehood, the gospel can not enter. Salvation is impossible. The soul will take no other gospel but the sophism, "Ye shall not surely die." But when the lie is abandoned, when the will adjusts itself to the truth, and the soul begins to see and feel that sin brings ruin and death, then the inquiry will naturally be made, "What shall I do to be saved?"

Lie No. 2.

When the power of the first great lie is broken, so that the conviction of the evil of sin is awakened in any measure, Satan is ready with this monstrous untruth — "*God is a hard Master, reaping where he has not sown, demanding service which no man can render, and therefore it is useless to attempt to obey him.*"

With thousands, the false impression is accepted as truth. The Bible says, "Love God with all your heart, and your neighbor as yourself." "Impossible," says Satan. "Love your enemies; bless them that curse you," says God. "No man can do it," insists the father of lies. "Obey the Sermon on the Mount," says Christ. "It is out of the question; no man ever did it," responds the adversary. "Overcome the world; stand up for Jesus against principalities and powers; die to sin and live unto righteousness," says the Word. "It is out of the question; Christians are no better than others," answers Satan.

Thus the debate goes on, till the falsehood is effectually rooted. Viewed through this lie, the gospel is only suggestive of perplexing doubts and fears. It disappoints hope, and involves the soul in a painful effort to obtain the good it never reaches; and the Christian seems a very Sisyphus, forever doomed to struggle to no purpose between the requirements of the gospel and the impossibility of performing them.

How effectually does Satan accomplish his malicious purpose with all whom he can persuade, consciously or unconsciously, to accept this falsehood! No man will truly embrace Christianity, as thus conceived.

But the falsehood is transparent. The gospel proclaims "liberty," not a "yoke of bondage." How completely is this device of the enemy refuted by the simple word of God!—"If there be first a willing mind, it is accepted according to that a man hath, and not according to that he hath not."

"Why, then, does it *seem* so hard for even many honest minds to perform Christian duty?" There is but one answer. They have linked their souls to some falsehood through which they can practically see Christ only "as a root out of dry ground." The object of love is hidden. The only way of escape is to abandon the lie, to cease to make Christ a hard Master by renouncing the lie that he is so. Cast away the word of Satan, which brings death, and lay hold of the truth, the simple fact, that God is the easiest, most considerate, loving, and sympathizing Master in the universe; that he will perform all his exceeding great and precious promises, and make his grace abound above all our necessities and infirmities; wrench the soul at once from the falsehood; stay it upon the truth, to live or die with that, and deliverance will come; new heavens and a new earth will appear.

Lie No. 3.

Another lie of this class is the bold falsehood, *that the sinner does not possess the natural ability to do what God requires.*

The former lie sets the mind to looking at God's commandments as grievous — too difficult for poor, weak human nature; not absolutely impossible to be performed, but so unreasonable as to discourage effort. This one, on the other hand, turns the eye within, to the alleged fact that the mind is not endowed with the power which is necessary to obedience. When the will is committed to this false persuasion, the consequences are well nigh as disastrous as if there were, indeed, no mental power by which obedience to God could be rendered. No man undertakes to do what he holds in his will that he can not perform.

I am not now reasoning with speculative fatalists, but with those to whom, having committed themselves, in spirit, to this falsehood, it *seems* as if they lacked the power to obey God; and it may facilitate their escape from this device of the enemy to look at the simple facts as they are. One fact is, that we can not serve two opposite masters at the same time. We have no ability to serve God *while we persist in serving Mammon*. But the requirement is, that we abandon the service of the wrong master, and enter upon that of the right one. We are not to accept the lie that we have no power to serve God at all, because we can not serve him, while we allow ourselves to be the servants of sin and Satan. Another simple fact is, that the power to choose, serve, and love one object, is a power so to devote ourselves to another. It does not require different powers of mind to serve different masters. Taking the truth, then, as it is in regard to God, — that he does not require what we can not render; that his "grace is sufficient for us;" that every thing in the universe, which is lovable and attractive, centers in him, and invites our love and service, — it seems infinitely absurd to say, we can not love him as he requires. Away, then, with the falsehood, the belief of which perverts the mind's powers, and let the soul be adjusted to the truth. It is not some great thing, requiring vast capabilities, which God demands, but simply to receive an offered and loving Savior, whose own efficiency will accomplish our salvation, while we render him the service of grateful, trustful hearts.

Lie No. 4.

"*There is no mercy for me.*" There are many, in all our congregations, who have given place to this falsehood. They have been through revivals; they have often sought a religious experience; they have struggled long against their sins; they have "done many things," and yet they are "without hope and without God in the world." The *feeling* that there is no mercy for them, has pressed itself upon them; they have yielded their wills to it as a truth, and thus closed the door against themselves.

But the falsehood is palpable. The testimony of God himself is, that "whosoever will" may "come and take the water of life freely;" that Jesus has "tasted death *for every man;* " that "*none* who come to him shall be cast out;" that where sin abounds, grace much more abounds; that he *has given* eternal life to men, so that it only awaits their reception by faith. Nothing can exclude a soul from heaven but a voluntary distrust and rejection of offered mercy. Let the lie, then, be dislodged, and the soul be adjusted to the truth as it is in Jesus, and mercy shall be found as abundant as ocean waters.

Lie No. 5.

"*I am not elected; or, if I am, I shall be saved at any rate; and if I am not, I shall be lost, do what I may. He will have mercy on whom he will have mercy, and whom he will he hardeneth.*"

This device of Satan, one would think, is too worn to have influence with any honest mind. It is not likely Satan ever saw the catalogue of the elect; and if he had, he would not report it truly. God has said, "He that believeth shall be saved;" and to believe is, therefore, to "make your election sure." God is the Creator and Father of all men; and he has no preference of some men, *as such*, over others. He elects all who will believe, love, and obey him. He is not willing that any should perish. Only believe: God will adjust the doctrines of Election and Grace.

Lie No. 6.

"*Experimental religion is all a delusion. A change of heart is a mere excitement, which soon passes away, securing no change of character. It is safe to risk all on a good, moral life.*"

Many intelligent persons have so committed themselves to this lie of Satan, that those most imperative words of Christ, "*Verily, verily, I say unto thee, Except a man be born again, he can not see the kingdom of God,*" have ceased to affect them. Admit that some persons deceive themselves; that there are "stony-ground hearers" who become excited on the subject of religion without really becoming "new creatures in Christ Jesus;" that some, who receive the seed in good ground, do, at times, under the pressure of temptation, "leave their first love;"—is there any decent reason for believing this broad denial of the reality of all vital Christian experience?

When the inebriate signs the pledge, and stands with the hosts of temperance, is his experience of joyous exultation a delusion, because such emotions do not last?

When a parent's loving kindness, tender forbearance, and patient sacrifice for a wayward, rebellious, and wicked son, have at last broken his proud heart, and brought him to his knees, confessing and renouncing his grievous sin, and the tokens of parental forgiveness and favor fill his soul with joy, is there nothing in his change of heart, because that emotion must and will soon subside? Was the prodigal's return to his father's house a delusion, because the festivities of the occasion ceased when the fatted calf was eaten? and was the prodigal still in the same moral state as when spending his substance in riotous living in a strange land?

Who does not see the object of Satan in fastening this lie upon the minds of men? and how surely he accomplishes his malicious purpose by it with all who consent to receive it as truth!

Lie No. 7.

We have met persons with this strange falsehood engraven on their hearts: "*God does not love me; I am beneath his notice; am nothing in his sight; and he will not turn aside from his infinite affairs to give any attention to such a mote or worm of the dust as I am.*"

O, how false is all this! Satan knows that every such word is saturated with falsehood. The venom oozes out at every letter. "God does not love you!" You are the very person he loves. You may say as boldly and assuredly, — "who loved *me*, and gave himself for *me*," as did Paul, for he has "tasted death for every man." "Nothing in his sight!" You are more in his sight than the whole universe of material works. For you they were made. For you his angels minister. For you he has prepared a mansion and a crown. He calls *you* to his throne, and to all the fullness of his own glory and blessedness. You are a chief object of his thought. To save you is his infinite affair; and from this object nothing ever diverts his attention.

Drop, then, the wretched falsehood, and lay hold of the truth that God is your Friend, your infinitely loving Father, who waits to be gracious to you. Away with the falsehood, that the greatness of God places him beyond your reach. If his infinitude does not prevent his "clothing the grass," or "numbering the hairs upon your head,"—if it does not prevent his creating and providing for innumerable orders of living existences, invisible to us except through the most powerful microscopes—surely it will not prevent his care for your immortal soul, the noblest specimen of his handiwork.

Lie No. 8.

"*I do not need religion; I am honest and sincere, and this is enough.*" This lie is strongly impressed on many who would shrink from its avowal. Perhaps the mass of men have no vivid sense of the importance to them of the Christian hope and life. The present life absorbs them. They are honest with the world; and, judging themselves by their human standard, which overlooks their relations to God, they fail to see their characters as the Bible presents them. They often conclude they are "as good as Christians," accept this falsehood of Satan, and dismiss the whole subject of personal religion.

This delusion ought to be dissolved by a moment's consideration of such queries as these: Have I not a future existence to provide for? Do I not need pardon for sin? Do I not need the eternal life which Christ promises to those who believe and obey him? Have I not a nature which is correlated to the nature of Him who made me, and which will not and can not be satisfied till it is brought into moral, spiritual, and eternal harmony with its Author? Have I no need of such a personal Friend as Jesus Christ? of the victory he pledges over sin and the grave? And do I know what I need as well as He knows, who said, "Without me ye can do nothing?"

We might extend this catalogue of Satan's lies indefinitely, for "their name is Legion." Every truth of the Bible which is directly important to the conversion of the sinner, seems to be contradicted or covered up in his mind by some false and deceptive impression. The Scriptures teach that the unconverted are "enemies of God;" that "the wrath of God abideth on them;" that their hearts are "deceitful above all things, and desperately wicked;" that "because sentence against an evil work is not executed speedily, therefore the hearts of the sons of men are fully set in them to do evil," as if they were presuming on the forbearance of God to live on in sin; that the unregenerate, supremely selfish heart is like a sepulcher, "full of all uncleanness and dead men's bones;" that he who willfully rejects Christ participates in all the wickedness of past ages; and yet these, and other similar teachings of the Bible, which, if a man believed them, would make him quiver to the center of his being, and humble himself in dust and ashes, are wholly without effect, because they are hidden from the soul by the falsehoods of Satan. All the exceeding great and precious promises of God to the penitent are, in like way, concealed from the sinner by the adjustment of his faith to the lies of the devil.

To one believing falsehood and not truth, conviction of sin is impossible; and the sinner vainly imagines that he shall stand acquitted before a holy God. Looking through the mist and vapor with which the adversary has enveloped his moral being, the whole subject of religion appears so complicated, so unsatisfactory, that he dismisses it as practically unworthy his attention. These dark clouds of falsehood must be dispersed before the Sun of Righteousness can be seen, or the soul be delivered from the guilt and ruin of sin.

CHAPTER XIV.

THE LIES BY WHICH SATAN AIMS TO WEAKEN AND WASTE THE INNER LIFE OF CHRISTIANS.

If it were possible, they shall deceive the very elect. — Matt. 24: 24.

It must be remembered that Christians are still moral agents, and susceptible to the influence of evil motives as well as of good ones. Their conversion does not remove them from the sphere of Satanic lies. If Satan could present his fictions and sophistries to Christ himself, much more can he urge them upon his followers. Falsehood accepted by the Christian will work as disastrously for him as for the unconverted. It may practically exclude saving truth from the soul, and, while it is believed, annul the whole power of the gospel.

Satan will aim to cripple the individual disciple, and to force him into a style of character and living which will not only destroy his usefulness, but make him a positive stumbling-block to the world.

God has been pleased to constitute his church the "light of the world and the salt of the earth." But she can be neither the one nor the other, except as she abides in Christ and the truth. Satan will, of course, seek to dissever that light and life-giving union, to turn her light into darkness, and to make her a false witness of Christ to men. Thus, by seducing the leaders into such a state of wickedness that they could only see, in Christ, "a prince of devils,"— a "fellow" unfit to live, — he extinguished the light of the Jewish church. And if now he would convert the church into a great worldly hierarchy, or into smaller and conflicting politico-religious organizations, working on a selfish basis in "the flesh," and not in "the spirit," it is because he hates the light, and would disqualify the church for effectual effort toward the salvation of the world.

We are now prepared to consider some of the lies with which Satan enters the fold of God.

Lie No. 1.

"*To be an active, effective Christian is very difficult; for you, it is impossible. You have not the necessary gifts, and are not called to it.*"

The enemy has effectually lodged this falsehood in the hearts of a very large proportion of the professed disciples of Christ. Their wills are adjusted to it as truth, and they have formed the habit of acting accordingly. A large majority of those who are found in the vestries and prayer-rooms, constitute a company of spiritual paralytics. Their tongues are dumb. They bear no testimony for Jesus, and they call not upon his name. If there be life within them, they give it no expression. They feel that they *can not*. There is a still larger number in the same bondage who seldom, for that very reason, visit the assemblies for social prayer and praise. They are quite as unable to use their talents out of the sanctuary as in it. They venture not upon a serious effort to win a soul to Christ, from the beginning to the end of the year. This is not true of unlearned and timid men, and men unused to public speaking alone, but of men of fine intellects, of disciplined minds, and of extended practice in the use of their powers, as well. Many feel their bondage sadly, and wish they were free; while others, believing the lie more implicitly, cease to condemn themselves, although they know they are most " barren fig-trees."

The consequences of believing this lie, this slander upon our blessed Lord, are terrible every way, to the individual, the church, and the world. The amount of talent, of moral power, which is, by this means, suppressed, is immense. If these buried forces were set free, and brought into earnest use, the whole world would soon feel their influence. There are individual men in the church, who, on other subjects, deeply impress and mold whole communities. If all Christian men used their talents for Christ with the same freedom and power which they show in their business, Christianity would speedily be elevated to its proper supremacy in the earth.

Then, one of the worst results of believing this

lie, is the practical difficulty which it puts in the way of maintaining communion with God in private. How can a child love a parent whom he regards as requiring service of him which he can not perform? No more can a Christian delight himself in a Savior whom he *practically* charges with laying upon him burdens grievous to be borne.

Christian, believe the lie no longer! God's commands are "not grievous." "Liberty to the captive" is proclaimed. "Out of the mouth of babes," Christ has ordained strength. Cling to the promise, "My grace is sufficient for thee." Resist the devil, hurling it into his face that *he*, not Christ, is the hard master. "Stand up for Jesus," lovingly to confess and praise his name, and he will loose your tongue; or, if that refuse to speak, your tears shall tell a story richer than words can express. *Persist, will it*, life or death, and you shall soon have possession of your powers, and the use of them for Christ shall make your soul, through grace, like a "well-watered garden."

Lie No. 2.

We class among the most mischievous lies of Satan, *his denial, to their felt experience, of the perpetual, loving, and sustaining presence of God with his people.*

The doctrine of the Bible is, that our God is ever present with his children, to comfort and sustain them in every hour of need. He knows their weakness and dependence, and pledges his presence to be the life and strength of their moral being. Under the old dispensation, his promise was to be with his people, " even down to old age and hoar hairs," and "in all places whithersoever they went." Paul takes the Old Testament pledge and makes it over, with increased emphasis, to the Christian church (Heb. 13: 5), as literally rendered in the hymn, "I'll never, no, never, no, never, forsake" thee. Moses rebuked the Israelites because they tempted the Lord, saying, "Is the Lord with us or not?" (Ex. 17: 7). His presence was not to be questioned, even in the wilderness. "Fear thou not, for I am with thee," saith Jehovah, in the Old Testament. "I will not leave you comfortless," "Lo, I am with you always," says Jesus, in the New. God's presence was specially pledged in the Tabernacle and Temple of the Old Testament; and under the New Dispensation, the Christian becomes the Temple wherein God dwells. The sum of the promises is, "I will dwell in them, and walk in them, and be a God and Father unto them."

Nor is this promised presence of God identical with the mere attribute of omnipresence. It is a conscious manifestation of himself to his people, whereby he communes with them, inspires them with his love, cheers them with hope, nerves them for endurance, evokes their gratitude, quickens them with his thoughts and purposes, persuades them to patient obedience, works in them to will and to do his good pleasure; and, in short, impresses upon them his own character, and fills them with his own fullness.

The strength of the Christian is, of course, in this conscious, loving, sympathizing, and upholding presence of God. With this, he can, with Paul, stand and do all things; or, with Moses, "endure as seeing Him who is invisible;" or, with the martyrs, shout victory at the stake. Nothing so effectually extinguishes the power of temptation as the conscious presence of God. We once knew a friend who was struggling against the habit of drinking. Passing daily the place of temptation, it seemed impossible to resist the burning appetite. His affectionate wife proposed to accompany him beyond the dreaded saloon, filled with old associates; and her loving presence was all-sufficient to counteract the temptation. And thus the abiding presence of God affords to his saints the infinite protection of his love.

On the other hand, without this sustaining Presence, we can not stand. So soon as Christ was removed from their sight, by seeming to fall into the hands of his enemies, all his disciples were overwhelmed. It was as if the ground had sunk from beneath their feet. The fearfulness of "that hour" and "the power of darkness" was all in the fact that, to their view, the presence of their Redeemer was taken from them. His departure involved the falling away of the very foundations on which their faith rested; and no wonder that they "all forsook him and fled." Had they known, then, what they afterward, on the day of Pentecost, learned, namely, that He, their God, was still present as their Almighty Spiritual Deliverer, they would not thus have fallen.

It is just as fatal to spiritual life, to-day, to lose our hold upon the conscious presence of our all-sustaining Redeemer, as it was in "that hour" when the "Shepherd was smitten" and the "sheep were scattered."

Now, if Satan can make the impression upon the minds of God's people that Christ is *not* continually with them as their life and strength, — if he can get them to accept the lie, even unconsciously, and commit the will to it as a truth, — he practically removes their spiritual foundations, and they sink like lead in the waters.

Just here, we think, Satan has gained his most material advantage over the church. To a large extent, his fearful lie is really, though not theoretically, accepted. The will of the Christian is *uncoupled*, as the train from the engine, from the truth and promise of the divine, conscious, all-sustaining Presence, and *coupled* to this terrible falsehood; and thus the enemy has him under his feet. We recognize the presence of God only upon occasion of revivals, perhaps, or when some great calamity or affliction arrests us; and the result is, we are practically overwhelmed with unbelief. Every thing is wrong with us; we are defeated, our arms and stores are taken, and we are prisoners of war. If Napoleon had fallen in the heat of a great battle, it would have weakened his own army and encouraged the enemy. Marshal Ney might have headed the column and rallied the French for victory. But if the "Captain of our Salvation" disappear from the field, our strength fails utterly. No Marshal Ney, no Gabriel even, could take his place. There can be no remedy for the loss of the Divine Presence. Horace said, —

"Nil desperandum, Teucro Duce," —

to express the unbounded confidence of victory which the army of Teucer had in their leader. Convert the line into a Christian maxim, and read it, —

Nil desperandum, *Christo* Duce, —

and you express exactly the feeling of Paul when he said, "I can do all things through Christ who strengtheneth me." Nothing is to be despaired of with Christ for our Leader. Cæsar said to his terrified boatman, as they set forth on the troubled waters, "*Ne time i vehis Cæsarem*"— Fear not; you bear Cæsar. If Christians had a faith enabling them to hear the Son of God saying to them, "Fear not; you bear your Savior: he who holds the sea in his hands and the winds in his fists is in the ship," they could no longer fear and be troubled, no matter how severe the storm. But if we lose our Leader, we are demoralized, and our strongest Peter strikes his colors at the taunt of a Jewish maiden.

What, then, is to be done? I answer, boldly resist the lie of Satan. Treat it as a lie, and not as a truth. Lay hold of the great Bible promise, and *insist upon its truth to you.* "But I do not *feel* his presence, but rather that he is far from me," you say. But what if you do *feel* so? Satan has anchored the lie in your sensibility, and, so long as you believe it, you can not feel otherwise. Are you to judge God by your feelings, or by his word? You do not *feel* that he is any where else; and is he therefore out of existence? You do not *feel* that his omniscient eye runs your being through and through every moment; that his power is exerted every instant to keep you in being; that he is a God of truth, and will keep his word to you; and will you make your feelings the *test* of God's character and attributes, and undeify him because your emotional nature does not recognize and respond to his presence? How can you *feel* his presence when your will *denies* it? You must cease to judge God by your *feelings*, and take hold of the *fact* as attested by his word and your own reason. Let God be true, and every man, and especially the Devil, a liar. Take issue with Satan; plant yourself firmly on the Word; fight the battle manfully in your sensibility, even "the good fight of faith," and you will not long be in doubt of his presence; you shall know it as the most precious of all realities in human experience.

Lie No. 3.

"*The promises of God do not belong to you,*" is another of the malicious falsehoods which Satan insinuates into the hearts of Christ's disciples.

The Bible is, substantially, a book of promises. It begins with the promise of a Savior, and ends with "whosoever will, let him come and take the water of life freely." These promises are among God's eternal *decrees*, to execute which, the whole power of his government is pledged. They are the coin of God's kingdom of grace, stamped in heaven, issued to men. They furnish the weapons wherewith the believer may conquer every foe. By them the Father speaks his own life to his children. These promises are given to all men to believe. God is no respecter of persons; and as he invites all to come and live, so he offers his promises to all.

Now, what does Satan attempt to do? He insinuates the falsehood into the hearts of men, that these promises do not belong to them! They believe him; professed Christians commit themselves to the lie; and the Bible becomes to them like a desert where are no springs, no streams, no trees, no flowers, no birds, no life, or rather, where all these exist only apparently, in the mocking splendor of the mirage.

Even Jesus, the central figure in the Bible, the very Tree of Life, on whose branches there is fruit enough for the "healing" of the nations, and in whom the promises are all "yea and amen," becomes as a root out of a dry ground, with no form or comeliness to attract the soul from the things which corrupt and destroy it. Up from the fountain of God's infinite benevolence, come welling the precious words, "Ask, and ye shall receive," "All things are yours," "How shall he not with him freely give us all things?" and yet many a thirsty soul is made to say, "Alas! they are not for me."

It is a lie, and nothing but a lie. They are for him, especially and specifically *for him*. He may as well say, the air he breathes, or the fruit he gathers from his orchard, is not for him. But he *feels* so; yes, because he accepts the falsehood. And thus the whole church is crippled by throwing away the promises of God.

But what is to be done? Done! There is but one thing that can be done. Away with the lie of Satan; resist it and him unto the death. John Bunyan says he had "many a pull with Satan for John 6:37, 'whosoever cometh unto me I will in no wise cast out.'" You may have many a pull with Satan when you claim the promises; but fear not; Jesus will give you strength. Break from the lie; stand by the Divinely-recorded, blood-sealed, and oath-confirmed fact, that the promises are yours; nor flinch for a moment, though your soul should quiver in the struggle like a ship strained through every timber in a hurricane. Stand by it, "though the earth be removed, and though the mountains be carried into the midst of the sea," and victory will be sure.

Lie No. 4.

"*At all events, the promises of God are not yours* NOW — *certainly not till you die.*"

This is an artful pretense of the adversary. The promises can avail us little in this our time of need, unless we may claim them *now*. This Satan knows; and if he can make this lie succeed, we are enslaved to him while on earth. Many seem taken in this snare. They have adopted the idea that religion is to save the soul from hell and sin in another world. They live here as other men do, and hope the promises of God will be fulfilled in their salvation at death. But we are required to live a new life *here*, to follow Christ, to be the "light of the world," to be "dead to sin and alive unto God;" and we can not possibly do this except as we are supported by the fulfilled promises of God. Let every Christian, then, cling to the promises for present, needed grace. God will be no more ready to fulfill the promise for pardon when death comes than he is now. He is as ready to give us all we need to-day, as he will be to give us the crown at the end.

Lie No. 5.

Satan often insinuates into the minds of Christians the falsehood *that the promises of God do not mean so much as they may seem to — that they are to be taken in a limited sense.*

The practical feeling of those who are ensnared by this device is, that the promise, "My grace is sufficient for thee," is only sufficient for some things, at some times. Grace will do something, but the world will, after all, have the mastery. They feel that they may, perhaps, have the presence of God at times, but do not expect him to abide with them; that he will save them from vulgar and gross sins, perhaps, but not that he will keep them "unspotted from the world," and give them the consciousness that their ways please him. In like way, all the essential promises are, by unbelief, brought down from their Divine meaning to a human standard. This is a subtle expedient of the adversary to dislodge the believer entirely from his hold upon God through his promises. If the Lord is not to be trusted to do *all* he engages to do, to fulfill his *whole* word, who can tell for what he may be trusted? Can we change the terms of God's promise, and then rely upon him to perform it? It is no longer *his* promise, but our substitute for it. If we change the promise, we give it all up; we dishonor God; we deny his attributes; we "limit the Holy One of

Israel," and "tempt the Lord." We shatter the foundations of our faith, and our confidence becomes a miserable presumption.

If men would not remain poor, withered, and dead branches of the Vine, they must abandon this falsehood. No such impeachment of God's faithfulness must be allowed. Rather, let every man accept God's challenge, and prove him, and see if he will not " open the windows of heaven, and pour out the blessing till there is not room to receive it;" see if he will not " do exceeding abundantly above all that we ask or think." Hold the promise *at par*, and never consent to its depreciation even to the fraction of a mill. Dishonor not God. His words are full of meaning. When he pledges you a " well of living waters," do not go as if you were burdening his benevolence, and ask for a single drop. " Open thy mouth wide, and he will fill it." We interpret no other friend after such a fashion. Nay, we would not acknowledge as an earthly friend, at all, one who would mock our necessities with large and glowing promises, only a tithe of which he would perform. Resist the subtle tempter, and cling to the Faithful Promiser, as sure to fulfill his gracious words " unto the uttermost." Find the promise your soul needs, and present it in confidence at the mercy seat, and it will be honored.

These will suffice, perhaps, for an illustration of the falsehoods by which Satan seeks to cripple the church of God. His lies are numerous, subtle, complicated. Each one must study his own case; and, seeing by what manner of falsehood the living word and the luminous face of Jesus are hidden from his view, he should resist it with a faith like Abraham's, and with supplication like Jacob's.

The lies of Satan often penetrate our theology and our philosophy, as well as our religious experience; and they all work toward hiding both our sins and our Savior from us; toward a self-righteous morality, instead of the righteousness which is of God by faith.

There are false sentiments, imbedded in the mind of the church, which are working out the greatest evils on a vast scale. Of these, perhaps none is to be more deplored than that which makes the Christian world feel that the children must be expected to grow up in sin, and be converted only in adult life. We have believed this, notwithstanding the warning of God to them, to "remember their Creator in the days of their youth, before the evil days come," and notwithstanding the special invitation of Christ that the little ones be brought to him, and in violation of all just views of the importance and power of early moral training. How subtle is this device of Satan, to gain time *to set* their characters in wickedness; to establish them in ruinous habits, and so to draw them into the whirl of life, that they will cease to think with any pleasure of the things of God!

CHAPTER XV.

THE FIERY DARTS OF THE WICKED ONE ILLUSTRATED BY A SKETCH OF A REMARKABLE CASE.

The shield of faith wherewith ye shall be able to quench all the fiery darts of the wicked one.— Eph. 6 : 16.

IN ancient warfare, darts, made of combustible material, were set on fire, and thrown at the enemy, with the hope that they would burn as well as kill. Paul, in his description of the Christian armor (Eph. 6:), urges the use of "the shield of faith, wherewith ye shall be able to quench all the fiery darts of the wicked one." We must, therefore, conclude that Satan uses some such burning missiles, doubly charged with moral evil, in his warfare against Christian believers. Illustrative of his fiery darts, we will first relate an anecdote of

"*Father Carpenter,*" *of New Jersey,*

a man wonderfully taught of the Spirit, who long since rested from his labors, after seeing thousands hopefully converted through his instrumentality. The facts were detailed to me by an elder in my church, who was himself a spiritual child, and an intimate acquaintance of Mr. Carpenter.

An excellent and conscientious woman, well known to a large circle of Christian friends, had, for twelve years, been weighed down to the earth with the conviction that she had committed the unpardonable sin. Her friends, who had been familiar with her history, were fully confident that she had done no such thing, and were greatly interested to help her out of what they believed was the snare of the Devil. They labored hard to persuade her to detail the circumstances by which she was led, as she supposed, to blaspheme the Holy Ghost; but none of them could prevail upon her to open the case. She felt that it was of no use, and she could not bring her mind to it.

At length, "Father Carpenter," hearing particularly of her case, and knowing beforehand her reluctance to tell the story of her fall, went to her house. He introduced himself to the lady, made known his errand, and then entered boldly upon his work by telling her *that she must relate to him all her religious history.* "O Mr. Carpenter, I can not do it," was her reply. "*Madam,*" said he, "*you have got to tell me. My Master has sent me here, and I shall never leave your house till you do. You shall board me till I die, or tell me all!*" Thus saying, he began to remove his over-coat and make himself at home. She saw and felt that he was in earnest, and finally, with a sigh, said, "Well, if I must, I must."

She went back to her early life, and traced her religious impressions up to a time when she thought she gave herself to her Savior, who then seemed to smile upon her and fill her soul with the joys of his salvation. Her feet seemed upon the rock, and a new song was in her mouth. She became interested, and labored for the salvation of others; was often in revivals of religion, and was evidently useful in the work of winning souls to Christ. Here she sighed again, as she related how, in the midst of a revival scene, and almost while praying for the conversion of sinners, she was overwhelmed with the idea, suddenly sprung upon her, that she had blasphemed the Holy Ghost. A voice within her, as it were, charged it upon her, and a rush of hateful and blasphemous thoughts confirmed the impression that the fatal deed was done. Her sensibility was pierced as with an arrow, and instantly her peace was destroyed and her hope blasted. It was a fiery dart. She yielded herself to the conviction that this was, indeed, the unpardonable sin, actually committed; and, for twelve years, she had been groaning in her despair.

Father Carpenter saw how it was. Satan had driven into her soul a fiery dart, which she had failed to repel with the shield of faith. The wound naturally created a revulsion in her emotions, and she *believed* the lie. She committed her will to it as a truth, and thus turned the key of her prison-house upon herself.

The good man saw that it would probably do no

good to reason with her. The only hope was to dislodge the falsehood from her mind. He therefore turned his back to the lady, and addressed himself to Satan after this manner: "O thou father of lies, thou accuser of the brethren! O thou god of this world, who dost blind the minds of men, and hide from them the face of Jesus Christ! O thou roaring lion, who goest about seeking whom thou mayest devour! O thou tempter of the Son of God! O thou murderer from the beginning! *wherefore hast thou kept this daughter of Abraham in bondage, lo, these twelve years? Come out of her, and let her go in peace!*"

While Father Carpenter thus boldly "rebuked the devourer," and, by faith, bade him release his prey, the spell was broken, and the good lady came out of her prison, shouting praises to God for her deliverance.

An excellent brother and officer in the church of Christ gives me the following account of the manner in which his own soul was pierced with the fiery darts of Satan. It happily does not appear that he yielded to the adversary, as did the lady in the foregoing account.

Before his conversion, and while he was earnestly inquiring after the Redeemer, he was stung with the thought, which was made to seem *his own*, that, so far from wishing to be a Christian, he was willing to make his bed in hell, and curse God forever, and sell his Savior for less than thirty pieces of silver. For weeks together, his mind was so pressed with blasphemous thoughts and feelings, that he could avoid uttering them only by holding his tongue between his teeth when the temptation arose. Then, as if to force him by argument to speak blasphemy, Satan confronted him with the feeling which seemed as real as life, that his eternal state was settled; that he was, as to his state of mind, already in hell, and might as well, at once, "curse God and die." He cried for help; and, as if to answer him, Satan, appearing as an angel of light, withdrew the multitude of his darts for a season, *giving him relief*, and so, relative comfort, and suggested that he might now indulge hope and believe himself a Christian! A ray of light from above exposed the trick of the deceiver, and showed him how easily he might, at that point, have begun building his spiritual house upon the sand! The danger he had thus escaped quickened him to cry out more earnestly unto God for his salvation. And now appeared his Savior, saying, "Thy sins are forgiven thee; go in peace." But the enemy pursued him still with his fiery darts, which, for a season, fell harmless at his feet. Coming, however, with great wrath, Satan seemed to say, "I will have you yet," with a voice so audible that his own tongue replied aloud, "No, you will not; for Jesus is my Deliverer." Even while he stood up to unite with the church, and enter into "the brotherly covenant," Satan made a final and desperate assault upon him, filling his mind with the most hateful and blasphemous thoughts toward God and his church, till it seemed to him as if he should sink through the floor.

For years, this brother was much of the time in the most intense agony of mind, weeping and mourning, and feeling as if he must die in the struggle. It was no marvel to him that Luther should hurl his inkstand at the head of Satan. The experience of such men as Bunyan and Baxter will readily occur to the reader.

There are many who suffer much from lustful thoughts and impure images, thrust upon them like darts, which both inflame and pierce the sensibility, and throw the mind into an agony of grief and sorrow. The enemy pursues them so relentlessly with this kind of weapon, that they often conclude that their hearts are too unclean for the Spirit to dwell in, and that they must abandon all hope in his mercy. They are ashamed to carry such things to Christ; they find it impossible to rid themselves of them, and they stand and suffer until God rebukes the adversary. They need to learn that the shield of faith is given them to quench even such fiery darts.

It should be said here, that these missiles sometimes drive men to insanity. The charge of blaspheming the Holy Ghost is adroitly thrust upon the soul; the will commits itself to it as true; hope dies, of course, and all seems lost; the brain becomes morbid, and reason gives way. It is not the result of receiving the gospel, but of believing Satan's lie. It is as illogical to argue from this against Christianity, as it would be to attempt to disprove astronomy by the insanity of one whose brain had been turned by too exclusive gazing at the stars.

CHAPTER XVI.

SATAN AS THE "ACCUSER OF THE BRETHREN."

And I heard a loud voice saying in heaven, Now is come salvation, and strength, and the kingdom of our God, and the power of his Christ: for the accuser of our brethren is cast down, which accused them before our God day and night.— Rev. 12 : 10.

The verse preceding that above quoted shows that this accuser was "that old serpent, called the Devil, and Satan, which deceiveth the whole world." The accusations of the adversary are, of course, false; but, if believed as true, they are as fatal, for the time being, as if they were true. If we include among them the lies of Satan upon which we have already dwelt, his accusations against Christ, his word and providence, made to the believer, we can not fail to see how the whole gospel must be effectually obstructed; and how, by the casting down of the accuser, "salvation, strength, the kingdom of God, and the power of his Christ," must be at once realized, both on the scale of the individual believer and of the world. To have any force with professed believers, the accusations of Satan must *seem* to come from God; and perhaps when it is said that Satan "accused them before our God day and night," it is meant, that he makes his accusations appear to the accused to come from God. It is a fact that he does so, and that this would fall in with his purpose; whereas, to make them literally before the Omniscient One would defeat his designs.

The accusations of Satan are numerous and subtle. Many most sincere and honest persons find themselves accused of wrong motives in their attempts to serve God. They would not for the world do wrong; their consciences are tender; they abhor wickedness in themselves and in others. The accuser steps in and insinuates that their motives are not right in the sight of the Holy One, and they can not, therefore, expect his favor. They accept the accusation, and go into condemnation, deprived of communion with God.

Sometimes Satan falsely accuses Christians of neglecting their duty to God, and thus breaks up their communion with him. You may find many a disciple with prostrate health, and with a burden of care in the family, which leaves no time or strength to visit the sanctuary, or scarcely the closet, or to read the Bible and pray at appointed seasons. Their weary bodies demand more rest than can be taken. Satan comes and accuses them with sinfully neglecting the daily worship of God. Not realizing the fact that, in spirit, they may worshipfully rest their wearied hearts upon him and be refreshed and quickened while they are bearing their heavy burdens, they heed the accusation as if it were from their Savior himself, and go into painful self-condemnation and reproach. They should see that the faithful performance of the daily duty he gives them, is acceptable to Christ, and, if performed for him, will not deprive them of his presence and grace.

Others are accused of such unworthiness that they dare not claim the promises. They admit the accusation as coming from Christ, and are insnared. Neither salvation, nor strength, nor the kingdom of God, nor the power of Christ, can come to them till the accuser is cast down, and they see that the gospel is for the unworthy.

Many are accused of sin in that they seem so much tempted to sin. Those who love sin are scarcely conscious of the difference between temptation and transgression. But in becoming Christians, men must renounce sin and set their hearts to resist it. Although this is done, Satan crowds temptation upon the soul, and then turns round and makes his accusation on the ground of so much temptation. Many excellent Christians are easily insnared by this means, because they do not properly regard the distinction between temptation and actual sin. We remember once preaching a sermon, the object of which was to draw out and enforce this important distinction. An English lady of much cultivation was greatly affected by the truth, and came out of her despondency into liberty, exclaiming, as she threw up her hands, "I have been in bondage all my life, because I have not, till now, understood the difference between being tempted to sin and sinning." The accuser, in her case, was cast down, and salvation and strength came to her longing heart.

Not a few are accused of having blasphemed the Holy Ghost. Ministers understand what is meant when their parishioners come and cautiously inquire what that fatal sin consists in, and how those who have committed it will feel. To believe the accusation is fatal, till the accuser is cast down.

Again: Christians are often annoyed and obstructed, in their religious life, by the accusation that their entire religious experience is a failure. "You were never sufficiently convicted of sin;" "You have never been thoroughly converted;" "You do not believe the Bible, especially its severe and discriminating doctrines;" "You have no evidence that you are a child of God;" "You are afraid to die." Thus the accusations run. Those who yield to them are full of uneasiness, and have no peace with themselves or with God. His salvation, strength, the kingdom and power of Christ, are effectually obstructed. Let the accuser be cast down, and a loud voice shall be heard from heaven proclaiming deliverance.

The Christian will say, "What is to be done with these accusations? I can not remove them." Satan intends by them to keep you from Christ. Defeat his purpose, then, by going at once to the Savior with them. If you doubt whether you ought not, and must not, in truth, condemn yourself, go *honestly* and *confidently* to Jesus, and ask him to search your heart. Do not judge yourself, especially by your feelings, but let Christ judge you. Be not accused away from him. If your will says, " Get thee hence, Satan," be not troubled, *only believe.* If the thousand and one suggestions and accusations by which Satan seeks to destroy the Christian's faith were *true*, he would not make them. He would seek other means of accomplishing his object. He does not aim to disturb the guilty with their sins, but rather to deepen their stupidity. But it *seems* as if the accusations were from the Holy Spirit, and must not be ignored. Let two things be remembered, then, in this connection: 1. The Spirit is never an *accuser*, but rather a gracious Friend, who draws his disciples by love away from sin to God. 2. It is never the intent or effect of his admonitions to repel the soul from Christ, and to keep it in darkness, in doubt, or distrust. Whatever has that tendency — as Satan's accusations have — is of the Devil, not of God. If the reader be embarrassed to determine whether the accusation is from below or from above, he may find the light he needs in Chapter XIX.

CHAPTER XVII.

WHEREIN SATAN IS CONSIDERED AS THE TEMPTER.

For this cause, when I could no longer forbear, I sent to know your faith, lest by some means the tempter have tempted you, and our labor be in vain.— 1 *Thess.* 3 : 5.

The deep solicitude here expressed, lest even apostolic labor should be rendered vain by the tempter, may well put all men upon their guard against temptation.

To be tempted is, indeed, a part of the Christian's inheritance. The disciple, in this respect, is not above his Master. Character must be tested at every point. We are to be winnowed and refined; our faith, our patience, our love, and our obedience, are all to be tried, that they may be " found unto praise, and honor, and glory at the appearing of Jesus Christ." Even the promises of God presuppose the conflict, while they pledge the victory over trial. They assure us that the floods shall not go over us, nor the flame kindle upon us (Isa. 43 : 2), though we must pass through them; that tribulation, which must come, shall work patience (Rom. 5 : 3) ; that a way of escape shall be opened to our faith out of every temptation, before it exceeds our ability to bear it (1 Cor. 10:13); that the Refiner's fire will only remove the dross (Mal. 3:).

Temptation has its uses. It develops men's characters, and brings them out as the light of the world and salt of the earth. We know Job best through his conflicts with Satan. We know the fidelity of Abraham, and the strength of his faith, through his trials. We know Daniel best in the lion's den; and his brethren in the furnace; and Bunyan in Bedford jail.

Satan does not, of course, solicit men to do evil as evil. He presents evil as good, and good as evil, and urges men to do only that which he seeks, by all possible and plausible disguises, to make them believe is right and good. He did not propose to Eve to do a wicked thing as such, but a thing by which her eyes would be opened, and she would be made wise. He appealed to her appetite for good food, to her taste for the beautiful, and to her desire for knowledge, and assured her that no harm would come of partaking of the prohibited fruit.

The forms of temptation, both to the righteous and the wicked, are innumerable. The lies, whereby Satan keeps men from becoming Christians (Chap. XII.), indicate the drift of the adversary's effort with unconverted men. He appeals also to their necessities, as he did to those of our Lord, when he was a hungered, and induces them to turn the "stones" of their integrity "into bread," by sacrificing it for gain. Alas! they forget to say, "It is written, Man shall not live by bread alone, but by every word that proceedeth out of the mouth of God."

He takes men also upon the wings of their imaginations, into the exceeding high mountain which overlooks the kingdoms of the world in all their glory, and excites their minds with visions of wealth, and fame, and power; and, thereupon, induces them to set their hearts supremely upon obtaining the alluring prize, thus bowing the knee in worship to him, and laying the foundation of their moral and spiritual ruin. They forget that it is written, "Thou shalt worship the Lord thy God, and him only shalt thou serve," and do not say, "Get thee behind me, Satan."

The Christian is often tempted to establish his discipleship by improper means, as Christ, his Messiahship. "If thou be the Son of God, command that these stones be made bread." In like way, Satan practically says to the disciple, "If you are a Christian, prove it by feeling as Paul did; by such an experience as Isaiah's, or Daniel's; or by doing some wonderful work, which will prove to the world that you are born again."

Satan also tempts the disciple, as he did the Master, to presumption. "If thou be the Son of God, cast thyself down: for it is written, He shall give his angels charge concerning thee: and in their hands shall they bear thee up, lest at any time thou dash thy foot against a stone." Jesus answered, "It is written again, Thou shalt not tempt the Lord thy God." We are taken in this snare whenever we cast ourselves upon the mercy of God, and do not, at the same time, sink our own will in his.

Another device of the tempter is to draw the mind of the disciple back under the power of old sinful habits. If a young Christian has formerly been an inebriate, or a covetous, or a proud, or a vain, or a willful, or a deceitful, or a peculiarly selfish man, — if he has been the victim of skepticism, of indifference and carelessness, or of evil companions, — he will have many a hard battle to fight with the tempter to avoid being swept down again under these old untoward influences. To gain a permanent victory here, will require all the *decision* of an honest farmer, of whom the following story is told, as well as all the divine upholding which he doubtless experienced: He had sold a large quantity of wheat to be delivered. The purchaser, relying on his well-known integrity, left him to measure up and forward the grain. While measuring it, as he filled the half bushel and struck it off evenly, this suggestion each time was thrust into his mind — "*Strike a little under, and you will save a bushel before you are done.*" He resisted it, of course, and still it kept coming. At last, the honest old man turned his head, and said, "*Satan, if you don't let me alone, I will heap the bushel every time.*"

With Christ for his Deliverer, let not the earnest

disciple fear the enemy: pirates do not pursue empty and worthless vessels.

Many of the devices of the tempter will be more strongly and vividly seen in the actual life of the tempted disciple, than by any formal statement of them; and we can not do better than consult the experiences of such a man as John Bunyan.

Bunyan was subjected to two long seasons of temptation, each lasting over two years. Speaking of the assaults of the tempter in these periods, he says, "My soul was like a broken vessel, driven as with the winds, and tossed sometimes headlong into despair: sometimes upon the covenant of works, and sometimes to wish that the new covenant and the conditions thereof might, so far as I thought myself concerned, be turned another way and changed. But in all these, I was as those that jostle against the rocks — more broken, scattered, and rent. O the unthought-of imaginations, frights, fears, and terrors, that are effected by a thorough application of guilt yielding to desperation! * * * I had cut myself off by my transgressions, and left myself neither foothold nor hand-hold among all the stays and props in the precious Word of life. And truly I did now feel myself to sink into a gulf, as a house whose foundation is destroyed. * * * These things would so break and confound my spirit that I could not tell what to do. I thought at times they would have broken my wits."

Hear also the man after God's own heart: "Thy wrath lieth hard upon me, and thou hast afflicted me with all thy waves; I am shut up; I can not come forth; I am afflicted and ready to die. While I suffer thy terrors, I am distracted. Thy fierce wrath goeth over me; thy terrors have cut me off."

After a season, in which he was so taken with the love and mercy of God that he could scarcely contain himself till he got home, Bunyan says, "I was much followed by this scripture: *Simon, Simon, behold, Satan hath desired to have you;*" and he thought the voice came to acquaint him that a cloud and storm were again coming upon him. "A few days later," he says, "a very great storm came down upon me, which handled me twenty times worse than all I had met with before: it came stealing upon me, now by one piece, then by another: first, all my comfort was taken from me; then darkness seized upon me; after which floods of blasphemies, both against God, Christ, and the Scriptures, were poured upon me, to my great confusion and astonishment." He felt as if he were possessed of the Devil, and were sinking in despair. The provocations which beset him seemed too terrible to be spoken of. The billows surged about him most fearfully, even when he attempted to worship God, and to fix his mind upon, and fasten himself to the truth. Satan would challenge and threaten him as with literal speech. The voice of the tempter rung in his ears, and seemed the very utterance of his own soul — " Sell Christ, sell him, sell him, sell him ; " and at length, weary of resisting, his heart seemed to say, " Let him go if he will ; " and down he fell again into the abyss of guilt and despair.

Then began a great strife of scripture against scripture in his soul. Trying to hold on to the promises, the threatenings would strike him like the lightning. If the gospel offered him comfort, the law, with its sharp sword, would strike it dead. If he would hope in God's mercy, the tempter would insist that he was but another Esau, who had sold his birthright; until, at length, the promise waxed stronger than the word of condemnation in his spirit, and Jesus showed him the precious words, *Mercy rejoiceth over judgment*, and gave him rest.

Thus the most fearful trials, and the most precious deliverances, mingled in the experience of Bunyan, till God had taught, and refined, and prepared him to give to the world his Pilgrim's Progress, a book second only to the Bible itself in its power to aid the soul in the escape from sin, and in the homeward journey to the Celestial City.

It is needless to dwell further upon the forms of temptation, as they are not material ; it is the victory over them which is important. It is unnecessary to speak of the bold and daring temptations whereby the Achans, the Gehazis, and the Judases come to head the calendar of crime. Such men are Satan's willing subjects, and do not wait to be inveigled, by subtle devices, into his service. Few Christians know as much of the severity of temptation as did Bunyan. If men were more in earnest to live out the full Christian life, and were *determined*, they would know more of the "depths of Satan," and of the heights and the glory of Christ's salvation.

Now, in view of all the schemes of the tempter, there is just one thing, on our part, to be done. To all his solicitations, come from what quarter they may, within or without, the soul must steadily and patiently answer, "No; I will not yield one iota from the will of God. God helping me, I will not knowingly swerve from his requirements, though I walk in darkness all the way to his judgment throne. I will not, by the grace of God, cast away my confidence, though the trial of my faith should last, like Abraham's, for twenty-five years; though, like Job, I should be bereft of all earthly comforts; or be reduced to a poverty like my Savior's; or, like Daniel and his brethren, the lion's den or the fiery furnace await me; or though, like Jesus, I must die an ignominious and cruel death, crying out in my despair, 'My God, my God, why hast thou forsaken me?' I will insist, with Bunyan, that neither guilt nor hell shall take me off my work."

This is the soul's true position before the tempter; and, in that sublime and glorious attitude, we will endeavor, in the next chapter, to show how the believer shall be effectually and gloriously delivered from the power and depths of Satan.

CHAPTER XVIII.

WHEREIN APPEARS THE CHRISTIAN'S DELIVERER. — METHOD OF VICTORY SHOWN.

For this purpose the Son of God was manifested, that he might destroy the works of the devil. — 1 *John* 3: 8.

For the battle is not yours, but God's. — 2 *Chron.* 20: 15.

WE have shown in the last chapter what is the true position of the believer before the tempter. The Christian and Satan are at issue. What will be the result of the conflict? Both are determined. Can the man stand against the Devil? Can *he* do it who has formed his habits in the enemy's service, and been his willing captive all his days?

Can he rely upon the freedom of his own will? Free agents are but too easily persuaded to abandon their right choices, and form wrong ones. The reformed inebriate is free, and yet, how weak he is when the flames of appetite kindle upon him. Peter was free, and strongly determined in himself rather to die than yield; yet how easily did Satan insnare him, and lead him on to deny his Master! The world is full of free agents, who ought to stand firm in a right will; yet what a mournful comment we have upon man's moral weakness, in the almost universal surrender of the race to the "lust of the flesh, and the lust of the eyes, and the pride of life"! The weaker will is easily persuaded by the stronger one; and Satan's is of superhuman energy. As some Napoleon will hold a nation under his almost omnipotent sway, and evoke all its resources, and subject them to his purposes, so Satan is able, by his vast power of will, to sway his scepter over a world of weaker minds, and to persuade them to enter his service and do his bidding.

Now, in this conflict of will with Satan, *no man will stand relying upon himself alone.* This is equally the doctrine of the Bible, of common sense, and of experience. A will mightier than Satan's is demanded before he can be vanquished. That all-conquering and all-sustaining will is Christ's.

How, then, does Jesus, the Almighty Deliverer, so invest our voluntary natures with his own, so complement our powers with his life, as that, in him, we shall be able to stand fast against Satan, and all the powers of darkness? This is the question.

It is certainly no part of Christ's plan to relieve us from the conflict by expelling the enemy from the field by physical omnipotence. God's purpose, in his church, is to achieve over Satan a great moral conquest worthy of himself — a conquest to which the grand march of events, as they roll and surge through the eras of history, advancing from the chaos of Satanic darkness and misrule to the light of the millennial day, shall abundantly contribute. We must be obedient to the Captain of our salvation, and "fight the good fight of faith." The solution of the question we are considering will be seen in the light of the following facts and principles: —

1. Mind is made to influence mind; and, other things being equal, the power of one mind over another depends upon its greatness and goodness.

The strength of the finite mind is not always in itself, but often in other related minds: that of the child is in the parent; of the wife, in the husband; of the friend, in the friend. A very instructive anecdote, illustrative of this principle, is the familiar one told of President Davies, of the College of New Jersey, and a poor victim of intemperance, of somewhat cultivated intellect, who had lost all hope of escape from the tyranny of his evil habit. When the latter despaired of any thing but a drunkard's grave and a miserable eternity, this good and learned man met him, and heard his sad lament. He said to him, "Sir, be of good cheer; you *can* be saved. Sign the pledge, and I will be your strength to keep it. I will be your friend; and, with a loving arm around you, I will hold you up. When your appetite burns, and you feel as if you must gratify it, come to my house, sit down with me in the study, or with the family in the parlor, and I will be a shield to you. All that I can do for you with my learning, my books, my experience, my sympathy, my society, my love, my money, I will do. You shall forget your appetite and master it." The tear of hope and joy had gathered in that despairing eye, and the astonished man replied, "Sir, will you do all that?" "Surely I will." "Then I can and will overcome." He signed the pledge; and as long as the president lived, he kept it. His strength was in the good will and noble qualities of President Davies.

Conceive, now, of our blessed and glorious Lord himself coming to the sinner, whom he has already convicted of his lost condition till he is in despair of salvation by his own righteousness, and saying to him, in a voice full of compassion and sweet as music, "In me is thy help. Behold in me the sinner's Friend. Trust in me; take my yoke, which is easy, and my burden, which is light. Come to me with all your sins, your infirmities, your ignorance, and your weakness, and I will give you rest. All that infinite knowledge, sympathy, power, and love can do for you, I will do. I will betroth you unto me in faithfulness, in loving kindness, and in mercies forever. My strength shall be made perfect in your weakness, and no weapon formed against you shall prosper. All mine shall be thine in joint heirship forever; and because I live, ye shall live also." Here, surely, is hope for the weakest; and with more than the enthusiastic assurance of the disciple of President Davies, may the sinner cast himself upon the promises of Christ, and know that, by the working of that infinite mind on his own, he shall be effectually redeemed from all the wiles and power of the enemy.

2. When the character of Christ comes to be revealed to the eye of faith, by the manifestation of the Spirit, the response in the believer's heart is, "Whom have I in heaven but thee? and there is none upon earth I desire in comparison with thee." The love of Christ becomes the absorbing passion of the soul, as with Paul; and the very dispositions of the mind are regenerated and winged for heaven. It becomes altogether possible to glory in persecution and tribulation, and to be made conformable unto his death, if so we may attain to more of the excellency of the knowledge of Christ, and honor his name.

3. When Christ reveals himself to his disciples in *his relations* to them, his power over the soul becomes still more significant and complete.

The inebriate was doubtless impressed by the known excellence of President Davies beforehand, but it could avail him nothing, till the good man manifested himself to him in the relation of a personal friend and helper. It was this which saved him.

So, when Christ *manifests himself* to his disciples personally, as their God and Father, as Husband,

Brother, Friend, Life, All; as enfolding them in his great, loving heart; as cherishing them as the very riches of his own inheritance; as identifying their interests with his own forever; when he makes all this real to their inner consciousness by the eternal Spirit dwelling in them, — why should they not exult with a joy unspeakable and full of glory, and in him be stronger than the strong man armed?

4. When Christ is thus manifested to us by the Spirit, his truth looms up before the mind as a living and irresistible power for our defense.

We necessarily interpret a man's words by his character and his attributes, as we apprehend them. If a king speaks, his words have a kingly meaning. In like way, we shall interpret the words of God. When he opens himself to us, he opens to us, also, the infinite meaning and force of his words, so that it is no longer a marvel to us that his word called the universe into being. We can see how he can speak to things that are not as though they were, how he can call the dead from their graves, and uphold all things by the word of his power. We have but to say to Satan, "*It is written,*" to strike him down as with a thunderbolt. The thing that is written, if we will know it, is as efficient and irresistible in our behalf as it was in the behalf of Christ in the day of his temptation, for it expresses the will, the purpose, the decree of the Almighty. The promises of God, in this way, are, to the believer, all alive and instinct with reality and blessing. Through them, we rise out of the bondage of sin into the glorious liberty of the children of God, into a participation of the divine nature, having escaped, through them also, the corruption that is in the world through lust. The promises are no longer dead letters; they are leaves from the tree of life, they are grapes from Eshcol, they are the wine, and milk, and honey of the kingdom. They are all yea and amen in Christ, opening fountains in the desert and rivers in the dry places. The word of the gospel is the very power and wisdom of God unto salvation. No enemy can stand against it, if faith insist upon the whole divine meaning thereof. To an unbelieving mind, the Bible is as if written in sympathetic ink, which remains invisible. But when brought before a mind all a-glow with faith and love, the writing comes out in clearest characters, and proves itself to be indeed "the word of God with power."

5. When Christ manifests himself personally to us, the soul finds its entire wants perfectly met in him; and this, in effect, removes that from the mind which Satan must find in us, in order to make his temptations *stick*. If a man is hungry, and knows not how or where to obtain the only proper food, he may be easily induced to eat "that which is not good." His excited appetite will make him corre-

spondingly susceptible to the offer of food of any kind; but, if his appetite is entirely satisfied with the true food, it will not be easy to draw him away after meaner supplies. If a man dwells in a garden abounding with every variety of luscious fruit, what temptation need he feel to eat the "apples of Sodom," the "grapes of gall," whose clusters are "bitter," and their wine "poisonous as the venom of asps"?

Man is constituted with wants, the supply of which is not in himself — wants imperative and ineradicable. His highest blessedness comes with that *good* which meets these fundamental necessities of his nature. In his natural state, man does not know and enjoy the supreme good. Sin hides it from him. He lifts up his voice, and inquires after it, saying, "Who will show us any good?" (Ps. 4: 6). The world may promise, but yields it not. Wealth corrodes and turns to dust. Honor is empty. Society is pleasant, but its level is too low. Knowledge answers only in part. Home, if it be home, refreshes some departments of our being while it lasts, but there is still a void. Curiosity carries the traveler round the earth, and his tears are but the bitterer that there are no more worlds for him to explore.

Nothing *can* satisfy man's capacious, hungry soul till there comes to him the heavenly vision, revealing to his moral and spiritual nature the Son of God, his Redeemer and Savior. In that brightness above the sun, astonished and delighted, he will exclaim,

"Eureka"—I have found it, I have found it. Yes, he has found it, and it is life, eternal life to his soul, the full and glorious complement of his being. He seeks no longer. The sea within him is at rest. As the lungs are satisfied with pure air, and do not ache for a better substance to fill them,—as the eye is satisfied with the pure light of heaven,—so the soul which has found Jesus, through his personal manifestation, has *all*, and wants no more. To please him, to honor him, to know him more and more, to follow and enjoy him,—this is enough. To find Christ is to find that life which is "hid with God," the life which even Satan can not destroy.

6. It comes to pass as a result of this revelation of God in Christ to the soul, that wrong motives lose their power over the mind, and right ones rise to their legitimate supremacy; and the will, thus, comes to stand against the tempter with something of heavenly firmness. The whole force of wrong motives is broken by the revelation which the mind now has of their utter folly, madness, and wickedness. On the other hand, in a revealed and present Christ, center all possible right motives. Of the strength of these motives, the will partakes, and the whole soul stands firmly and without fear, rejoicing in the Lord and in the power of his might.

7. When the soul comes to abide in the Deliverer,

and to behold all things from that stand-point, we shall find all manner of agents and agencies folding their strong arms around us to sustain the will in its true position. It were enough, indeed, that God, with his infinite mind, should enfold and shield us; but he is pleased to make his saints and angels ministering spirits to each other, and all his works to praise him in the hearts of his children. The strength he gives to each is available for all; and that which he bestows upon all, for each, according to the measure of faith. The world, to the true believer, is full of the glory of God. There is, indeed, music in the spheres. The eye of faith, in a pure heart, sees God in all his works. He looks upon them from the sun; his heart beats upon them in the tides; his hand touches them in the breeze; his voice salutes them from the sky, or, still and small, whispers answers of peace from the unseen, but mighty forces by which he makes his will felt "from the center to the utmost pole of things;" and the aroma of his love is exhaled from all his works.

The things which were before a snare to them shall now minister to the advance of his people in holiness. Their wealth, consecrated to him and used to bless the world, shall bring rivers of blessing to themselves. Even the "cares of the world," borne for Jesus, shall not "choke the word," or render it unfruitful. Even Satan himself shall be made to contribute to their growth in grace; and they may well and triumphantly exclaim, "Who shall be able to separate us from the love of Christ?" The persuasion of Paul that *nothing* could do it, was most just.

8. But, in the final emergency of the conflict between the believer and the tempter, if, by any means, the adversary has succeeded in confusing the mind of the disciple, and has wearied him, almost to exhaustion, by a long siege of temptation, so that he is ready to give up in despair, — if he have cut and thrust him sorely with the sword of Apollyon in the valley of the shadow of death, — in that pregnant moment, clear to the eye of Omniscience, when the will can bear the strain no longer, the divine, almighty volition of Jehovah shall issue again, as when he said, "Let light be," and light was, and strike down the tempter quicker than thought, and deliver the prey, whose pent-up sorrows shall be changed to exulting praise, thanksgiving, and the voice of triumph.

Such we understand to be the method and work of Christ in delivering his disciples from the power of the tempter. Happy will he be whose faith shall enable him to persevere, till, in the progress of his experience, he shall have appropriated to his undying soul all the fullness of the blessing of the gospel of Christ.

CHAPTER XIX.

SATAN AS TRANSFORMED INTO AN ANGEL OF LIGHT.—PASTOR'S SKETCHES.

For Satan himself is transformed into an angel of light.—2 *Cor.* 11 : 14.

THE Bible teaches that Satan, for the prosecution of his malicious ends, assumes the guise of truth and goodness. There is a necessity that he should do so, in order to any success in his work. The human mind is made to be influenced by what is true, and repelled by what is false. Lies, therefore, to take effect in minds not wholly debased, must appear to be truths, and Satan must be a seeming angel of light.

It is in this character, we need most to be on our guard against the fell destroyer. If some one were plotting only our temporal ruin, through his angel manifestations, the knowledge of the fact would arouse our most indignant apprehension and watchfulness.

Let us attempt to expose Satan in some of his devices as an angel of light.

1. He holds before us *our happiness* as a motive of action. He knows we are made for happiness;

that we crave it through every susceptibility of our natures as the chief good, and that no appeal to us will find a more hearty welcome. By this means, he was successful with Eve. He assured her that the forbidden fruit would open her eyes, and secure to her the blessed experience of the gods. With the same plea, he urges on all men in ways of disobedience. His argument with them runs thus: "You are made for happiness; set your whole heart upon gaining it; the earth is full of good; seize it and make it your own; fill your coffers with wealth, for there is great joy in it; seek honor of men, for it is sweet; gratify the bounding impulses of the natural life, and one long gala-day shall be yours."

By such "fair speeches," he deceives the hearts of men, and leads them in a path far removed from that trodden by the self-sacrificing Savior. Satan conceals the fact that *real happiness* can only result from the conformity of our will to the will of God, and that the attempt to gain it by direct and selfish effort, is the sure way to lose it, and to involve the soul in moral ruin, although the *pleasures of sin* may, for a season, be enjoyed.

2. He appeals to their sentiment of charity and liberality to lure men on in the path of moral ruin.

Bigotry and intolerance are hateful. Charity is a heavenly virtue indeed, and liberality is beautiful as sunlight; but they are capable of perversion. Why should not this arch enemy of man play the angel of light after this manner? "Be charitable in your judgment of human sinfulness; there is much that is good in human nature; the philanthropists are noble-hearted men, and must be accepted of God; even the worst men often have many redeeming traits. Be liberal; he that believeth shall be saved, and it is not material that he should believe one creed rather than another; do not put too rigid an interpretation on the penalty of God's law, or the threatenings of the Bible. God is too good to punish the wicked, for he knows their weakness, and remembers that they are dust. The age demands a liberal Christianity."

Satan can make all this appear plausible enough to men who would like to have it so, and thus insnare them. But, by the same charitable and liberal reasoning about civil law, he might say to the murderer, "Do not think your life in peril from the law; the lawgiver is kind and merciful; he knows your infirmity, and will consider your temptation; you only sought your own good; you needed the money of your victim; you only shortened his days, for he would soon have gone to his grave; you have done many excellent things; your impulses are generous; fear not, charity will prevail, and you will not be condemned." Nor will this liberal reasoning apply any better to natural law. It will not do *charitably* to conclude that no harm will come of eating arsenic, or drinking prussic acid, or dropping a few sparks into the magazine. Such liberality would be inevitable death. The laws of God have an exact and changeless significance, which we can ignore only with infinite peril. There is a true doctrine of liberality, and we love it, and hate bigotry as, we believe, God hates it. But when Satan appeals to that noble sentiment to cheat the soul into putting light for darkness and darkness for light, and into substituting what men, in their pride and rebellion, wish to have true in the place of God's revealed word, we must cry out, *Beware*, lest you be found fighting against God, and tampering with the only possible grounds of salvation.

3. Satan, as an angel of light, makes abundant use of Scripture. The Bible is the great authority of the Christian world, and the adversary will use it with all the skill and cunning of which he is master. He will thrust in upon the mind, in its most impressible moods, certain fearful passages, forcing them upon the attention, after the manner of God's Spirit, for the purpose of destroying hope and confidence. Alas! how many sensitive souls has he cast down with such texts as these!—"There remaineth no more sacrifice for sins;" "He that shall blaspheme the Holy Ghost hath never forgiveness;" "He is joined to his idols, let him alone." Sometimes he will quote the Scriptures to keep men at rest in their sins: "No man can come to me, except the Father, which hath

sent me, draw him," is used to quiet sinners in their passive indifference, whereas it should stimulate them to search eagerly after the truth and the spirit whereby God does draw men to Christ. What an onset did Satan make upon the faith of many professed Christians, a few years ago, by leading them on, by false interpretations of prophecy, to risk every thing upon the doctrine that the world would surely come to an end, on the 23d of April, A. D. 1843!

4. Satan, as an angel of light, doubtless mingles, not a little, in revivals of religion. He does not oppose religion. He knows that man has a religious nature, which will express itself in worship. The more zealous he can persuade men to be in the service of false divinities, the better is he pleased; for the probabilities that they will inquire after the one living and true God will be correspondingly diminished. He is no enemy to religious emotion, if it shall be excited in his way. He does not object to his subjects rejoicing in the crowns they hope to wear, the harps they expect to play, and the golden streets they hope to walk, provided he can retain them in his willing service.

There is great power in a religious excitement. In such times, Satan will labor to satisfy men with a mere hope of pardon, without the new birth. He will turn the mind away, if possible, from the true idea of religion, of God's character, of sin, repentance, and regeneration, in order to make men build their houses on the sand, and not on the rock. We will introduce here, as illustrative, a

Pastor's Sketch.

In a season of religious excitement in a Western town, a man came to me from another denomination, and said, excitedly, "Sir, can you tell me whether there is any way in which I can come to understand my relations to God, and intelligently adjust whatever is wrong on my part toward him, so that I may know that there is harmony between us; or, have I got to be put into this revival mill, and be ground out a Christian, without knowing how I became or how I am to continue one? I am exceedingly anxious to know, for I have been through the mill five or six times, and my religion has never lasted me over six months. I am sick of it; and I came to you to see if I could find out a better way."

I was greatly interested in the inquiry and the spirit in which it was made, and replied thus: "God is the most intelligent and reasonable being in the universe. The controversy he has with you is definite, and, on his part, infinitely just. He has given you reason, and wishes you to follow its honest dictates, which will be found to correspond with his word. There is no manner of doubt that he wishes you to understand exactly where the controversy hinges, exactly what he wants of you, and why he wants it; and that, too, that you may deliberately and intelligently determine whether he is right, and whether you will, in view of the reasons he presents, at once become reconciled to his will, and earnestly devote your life, henceforth, to its honest performance."

His face grew radiant as this was said, and he then begged me to show him the way. I gave him the instruction any one would anticipate after reading these pages. He waited, thenceforward, on my ministry with open eyes and ears, in which, of course, many things were said for his special benefit. At length, at the close of a Sabbath, he gathered his family around him, and, with the Bible in his hand, said to them, "Half of my life has passed away, and I have not understood for what end I was made, or how I ought to live. Thus far, I have had no other idea in life but to do my own pleasure, and secure my own happiness, here and hereafter, if I could. I have been a purely selfish man. It has been no part of my purpose in life to seek to know or do the will of Him who made me. I have now settled it in my mind to live so no longer. I design to begin, at once, to do my Maker's will, and to trust him to do with me as he pleases, now and hereafter. Here is his word, in which he bids me give him my heart, my family, my possessions, myself, my all. Here, too, I learn that he answers the supplications of his people, and teaches them his will. I propose, now, therefore, to consecrate myself, you, and my all to Jesus, and to begin to pray that I may know and do his will."

He read the word, not knowing or anticipating what should follow. He closed the book, and turned and bowed by his seat to pray. As he knelt there, Jesus seemed sitting in the chair, waiting to fold his arms about the coming disciple. Those who know Christ can imagine the rest. That man was now a new creature understandingly; and, henceforward, his course was that of the living Christian, onward and upward.

5. As an angel of light, Satan often leads men into an intense devotion to moral reforms, while yet the heart is alienated from God.

A Christian brother once asked our opinion of the character of a professed disciple of Christ, whom he thus described: "He is a physician, worth seventy thousand dollars. He is outspoken in favor of all reforms, including those most unpopular. He is ever ready to pray, and to make religious exhortations. He advocates and urges the highest standard of Christian attainment. He will not commune with slaveholders. Yet, rather than give a poor widow her doctor's bill of five dollars, he will let her last cow be sold to pay it. Is he a Christian?" Our answer was, "It is easier to account for his outward religious conduct on the supposition that he is still in his sins, a supremely selfish man, than to account for his exactions of the poor widow on the supposition that he is in heart a follower of Christ."

It is to be feared that there are "reformers," who, standing upon the law rather than the gospel, — upon Sinai rather than Calvary, — forgetting that God is now seeking, by love, to win and save the lost, rather than by the terrors of justice to overwhelm them, — denounce transgressors with a bitterness of spirit which can only work wrath, never repentance, in the guilty. And thus they are themselves the captives of Satan as an angel of light; friends, "in the flesh," of justice, but, "in spirit," alienated from "the higher law" of mercy. Let those also beware of Satan's devices, who, on the other hand, commit a not less grievous offense, by indulging in a bitter retaliation against reformers, which naturally places them in the attitude of apologizing for the crying sins at which reform is aimed.

6. Satan often leads men into a most rigid conscientiousness in regard to some particular sin, while the heart is retained in manifest rebellion against God. It is not difficult for this false angel to appeal to the conscience, and arouse it, self-righteously, against some one form of wickedness. The Jews gave themselves credit for their rigid observance of the Sabbath, while their hearts were full of murderous hatred to

Christ. There are thousands who accept the false light which comes from the devotion of the conscience to some form — to almost any form — of external righteousness, while their hearts are full of selfishness, and all wrong in the sight of God.

7. On the other hand, Satan plays the angel of light by insisting upon "a religion of the heart — a spiritual religion. Works are nothing in the sight of God, who looks upon the heart. Only believe, and all will be well." Thus the adversary would satisfy men with an affectation of religion in the heart, — with a spurious faith which does not involve obedience, — while they may lack common honesty in their dealings with their fellow-men. Prayer is good; praise to God, well sung, is beautiful; but false and empty words, unaccompanied with works of obedience, reveal a kind of spirituality which is but the mockery of fools.

8. This false angel has a way of cheating men by inducing them to accept and contend for a "religion of principle." When our religion is one of true moral principles reigning over us, it is indeed beautiful, effective, and well pleasing to God. But the game of Satan is to cheat the soul into the mere holding of truth as principle in the *intellect*, while he retains the *heart* in his service. He is quite willing men should "hold the truth in unrighteousness," as

a theory of the understanding, while, as a law of life and duty, it is practically rejected; and this is an ungodliness against which the wrath of God is revealed from heaven — a wrath all the more terrible, because, knowing the truth, glorying in it, and contending for it, the soul refuses to obey it.

9. A very common method of the angel of light with timid disciples, whom the Spirit would especially draw into closer fellowship with the Father, as well as with nine tenths of those who desire to know what they shall do to be saved, is to present something short of Christ himself, as the soul's support and life.

The Jews were not different from other men in wishing to see a "sign." Every mind wants a resting-place, and necessarily desires to have it revealed, or signified. The Jews only sought the wrong thing. Christ himself was the proper sign unto them, but him they would not receive. Not unfrequently Satan himself dispenses "signs" to those who seek them, and satisfies them with a most false security.

As illustrative of many cases, we present another

Pastor's Sketch.

A very intelligent lady, who had been spending some months in my parish, came to me with her spiritual difficulties, seeking relief from long continued bondage and darkness. She was a professed Christian, but was in utter uncertainty as to her acceptance. For months, the great problem with her was, Am I a disciple of Christ? Till that was settled, she did not see how she could claim the promises, for, perhaps, they did not belong to her. She was repelled from the mercy-seat; her sins pressed her with their full weight, for she knew not that they were forgiven her. She dare not touch a drop of the water of life, though rivers of it were breaking forth in the desert around her. Thus the gospel availed her nothing, the work of the Spirit was arrested, and all was gloom and darkness.

"What you want, then, is evidence that you are a Christian," I said. "Yes; if I had that, all would be well." "How long have you been *seeking after this sign* of discipleship?" "A long time — nearly ever since I thought I was converted." "You need a sign, doubtless; and I suppose you can have one, even the best one: what will satisfy you?" "I do not know; something which will settle it in my mind that God has accepted me." "Well, suppose the Lord should speak to you from heaven, waking you from your sleep, and say, 'M——, your name is in the book of life; you are my child;' or suppose he should shed abroad in your heart such a sense of his love as you suppose he only grants to his children; would you be satisfied?" "O, yes; that would be enough." "I see what you want — something on which to rest your weary soul. You are tired of your struggle. I sympathize with you. Thank God, there is a rock on which we can plant our feet. But do you think you could long rest on your vision of the night? The voice might seem in the morning like a dream, and you might be tempted to doubt whether it came from God at all. Could you rest any better upon the wave of love that might roll over you, and lave your sensibility so refreshingly? Could you rest upon it after it was gone? It would be pleasant to remember it, but it could not be a rock under your feet. You need something which will abide with you, 'the same yesterday, to-day, and forever.' You are seeking after the wrong sign. There is a better one. Your Heavenly Father wants you should have the best. Shall I tell you what it is?" "Do, certainly." "*Well, it is Jesus Christ himself.* He is here, waiting and offering himself to you, to be the home, the resting-place, the asylum, the refuge, and stronghold of your soul forever. His ability and willingness are infinite. *He is the sign unto you.* He signifies pardon to you. He signifies God's infinite love and mercy to you. He signifies eternal life to you, for it is in him. He signifies the promises to you, for in him they are all yea and amen. He signifies your salvation to you, for he has given his word, and sealed it with his blood, that 'whosoever cometh unto him he will in no wise cast out.' He signifies every thing to you, for, 'in him dwelleth all the fullness of the Godhead bodily.' Let him be your sign, then. Put every thing into his hands, and rest your soul upon him for all. Do his will; follow him lovingly and trustfully, and he will give you rest and peace. It is simple. It is as when the bride accepts the offered bridegroom. She looks *at him*, and trusts herself *to him*, not to the wedding ring, or any thing else he may give her afterward. She takes him to her heart, and *with him* she is *satisfied*. He signifies all she wants. She delights to sup with him henceforth, but she thinks little of that, so satisfied is she *with him*. She wants no *evidence* that she has a husband, for she has the husband himself, which is better.

"My advice to you, then, is, to let every thing else go, as of no account, and simply receive this offered and waiting Jesus to your heart. He knocks, and waits to come in. Shall he come? Shall he? Shall he now?" After a short pause, with her head resting upon her hands, she answered, "Yes; welcome to my Savior — welcome." We went to the mercy-seat; Jesus entered. There was a great calm. The sky was clear. The darkness was gone, and the doubts forgotten. She wore a radiant face, and was ever after "so glad" that she came to ——, so dismal before, so pleasant now.

Reader, if you wish a sign, let it be your Savior.

CHAPTER XX.

HOW TO DISTINGUISH BETWEEN SATAN, SO TRANSFORMED INTO AN ANGEL OF LIGHT, AND CHRIST, THE TRUE ANGEL AND MESSENGER OF GOD, WHOM SATAN COUNTERFEITS.

If thine eye be single, thy whole body shall be full of light. — *Matt.* 6: 22.

THE practical importance of this topic is great every way. It must be so to all classes of men; for it appears, from the previous chapter, that Satan carries on his counterfeiting on a great and systematic scale. Those who ignore his existence, or who suppose themselves, in the main, exempt from his influence, or those who are not accustomed to watch for his devices, are all the more exposed to being led astray by Satan, as an angel of light. There are many who have little hope of discriminating between the false and the true, Satan and Christ; of knowing, with any assurance, what their own characters really are in the sight of God. They do not expect to gain the experience of Enoch, and have the testimony that they please God. Their minds seem paralyzed by the difficulty of finding out what the way of life is. They are oppressed and stumbled by the conflicting religious opinions of the world, and even of the churches, and have practically given up the contest for the truth, at this very point, and become hopelessly insnared. They seem to themselves environed with insuperable difficulties, growing, perhaps, out of their own natures, or the supposed obscurities of revelation, or the impracticability of applying any of the tests of which they have knowledge, so as clearly to expose the counterfeits of the adversary, and reliably to establish, in their convictions and in their experience, the genuine truth as it is in the Lord Jesus Christ.

It seems to the writer, that not a few are so despairing on this subject that it is even painful to have their attention called to it. They are in the condition of those slaves who would give all the world to gain their liberty, but, having no hope of gaining it, can not bear to hear or say a word on the subject to awaken discontent, lest their hard master should tighten the cords of their bondage, and make their case the more intolerable. They are afraid to look the subject in the face, lest their spiritual status should be damaged rather than improved thereby.

Can we then reasonably hope to distinguish clearly between the devices of Satan, as an angel of light, and the truth, as it is in Christ Jesus our Lord?

1. It would be infinitely unreasonable to suppose that God had required us to *obey him*, and that he had made no adequate provision for our knowing his will. This would be to require of us an absolute

natural impossibility. It is not conceivable that voluntary obedience should be rendered to an unknown command. Nor could a more unreasonable or blasphemous thing be said of God, than that, on pain of his eternal displeasure, he requires obedience to a will which he is slow to reveal. Is he a worse tyrant than Caligula, who posted his laws so high that the Romans could not read them, and then punished them for disobedience? How could our Savior invite us to hold fellowship and communion with him, and proffer us protection from the adversary, and yet leave it impossible for us to distinguish between that adversary and himself?

2. The Bible clearly teaches that we may know the will of God. It is itself a revelation of his will. His commands are distinctly and numerously spread out upon its pages. One great object of the incarnation, also, was, that men might have before their eyes a living and perfect embodiment, an exhibition, not merely in words, but in act, in life, and in spirit, of the will and character of God. Then, the mission of the Holy Spirit, who is promised for the honest asking, is to make known the will of God to men, to show them the truth, by which they shall be sanctified and fitted for heaven. The Spirit is well able to unmask Satan as an angel of false light. We have the promise of God also that, "If any man will do his will, he shall know of the doctrine;" and,

again, "If thine eye be single, thy whole body shall be full of light;" and, again, "If any of you lack wisdom, let him ask of God, that giveth to all men liberally, and upbraideth not; and it shall be given him."

3. It does *not* appear that it would be reasonable to expect God to force upon men the knowledge of his truth and will in spite of their unwillingness to receive it, — at least, not further than to fix so much light in the mind as would be necessary to moral obligation, and to the gaining of additional light, provided one should become willing to accept and follow it. This measure of light he has given to "every man that cometh into the world," through his reason and conscience, and has displayed his "eternal power and Godhead" in his works, so that all are without excuse if they do not obey him, and follow on to know his will more and more perfectly. But if men rebel against the light they have, and become "unwilling to retain God in their knowledge," then he may justly give them up to their love of darkness and to the dominion of their lusts.

Rejected truth is the rock which falls upon sinners, and grinds them to powder.

4. It does *not* appear that benevolence would require that God should make his will and truth known to us, even when obedient, without an effort on our part to find it. Perhaps he could not do this

except by endowing us with omniscience. Even the angels do not gain knowledge without study. They are represented as inquiring into the meaning of the prophetic utterances concerning the sufferings and glory of Christ. The prophets had to search diligently for the very truth they were inspired to proclaim (1 Pet. 1 : 10).

Nature nowhere teaches that we can know all the truth we need to know, without diligent and patient inquiry. Some things lie upon the surface, both of nature and revelation, but there are more things which lie deeper and require study. It is only by careful and minute investigation that the chemist comes to understand the composition of even common substances; and only by repeated and laborious experiment, that the natural philosopher can explain the working of the forces of nature. The Bible, too, is a mine, the full exploration of which requires patient and long-continued effort.

Good and evil are strangely mixed, and it is not always easy to separate them. Every good thing is so sure to be counterfeited, that all have occasion to take heed. We always assume the possibility of distinguishing between the true and the false, and the obligation to do it. It is in religion only as in other things. The gold can be separated from the sand, but it requires a process of washing and sifting.

Let us, then, proceed to inquire, how we can distinguish between Satan as an angel of light, and Christ, whom he counterfeits.

1. Take home the fact, and know it well, that Satan *is* a counterfeiter — that he does, indeed, appear and work for our destruction as an angel of light. It is not enough, therefore, to consider him as the inspirer of lust, falsehood, and crime. We are not to expect him to exhibit himself always in his true colors. We must regard him as seeking to promote his ends by what seems very angel-like, very beautiful in appearance, very promising to our happiness, very creditable to our reputations, very captivating in our experiences, very useful to our interests, very flattering to our hopes, very pleasing to our pride, and very honorable, apparently, to our God.

2. Consider the one great test by which we can distinguish between Satan as an angel of light, and Christ, whose mission he seeks to usurp. *Whatever leads to, or allows of, the setting up of our will against the will of God as the supreme law of our life and conduct, — whatever goes to promote a beautiful and correct exterior, while the will and heart are left enslaved to selfishness, no matter how righteous the forms of that selfishness may appear to ourselves or to men, — is of Satan.* On the other hand, *whatever leads to the complete surrender of our will, our life, and our all to God; whatever inclines us, in the bitterness of trial and sorrow, to exclaim, " Not my will, but thine, be done; " whatever makes us hungry for truth and righteousness; whatever persuades us not to*

make account of our external conduct, right though it be, but to glory rather in the moral beauty and excellency of our Savior himself, — *all this is of Christ, and not of Satan.* Jesus aims to destroy our selfishness, and make us partakers of the divine moral nature; Satan seeks to hold us in our sins, wearing his moral nature, and merely to satisfy us with a righteousness, beautiful it may be without, but rotten at the core.

The test does not seem a difficult one to apply. It does not require great learning, or extended experience, so much as a simple, and honest, and truthful heart. It only requires that the disciple should be faithful and watchful; for he who is true to the Divine voice within shall have his "senses exercised to discern both good and evil."

3. A primary question for the reader to consider is this: Do you want to know the distinction between Satan as an angel of light, and Christ the true Light, or *are you willing to be cheated?* Do you love darkness rather than light? If you are willing, on *any* conditions, to be cheated, there is no help for you. Satan will quite willingly accept your conditions. Your feet have slid already!

You can be honest with yourself in this matter, and with God; and you can know that you are so. If a man offers you a suspected note, and you propose to examine it by the detecter, he can not fail to know whether or not he wants the true character of the bill exposed. You can welcome the searching eye of Omniscience to penetrate your inmost soul. A young man once said to a minister, "Sir, you *hurt* me yesterday with the truth. You touched a very sore spot; but to-day I do not think you could hurt me, for it seems to me now, by the grace of God, that I am as honest with myself as I can be at the day of judgment. I welcome the light."

I beg the reader not to pass this subject indifferently. Stop. Reflect. To triumph here is to insure the great, eternal, and glorious victory, — to escape hell and secure heaven.

4. The great source of our ability to detect Satan as an angel of light, lies *not in ourselves*, not in our unaided powers, our superior wits, or keener sagacity, but *in Jesus Christ* himself dwelling in us and giving us the advantage of the light which is in him. The merchant's ability to detect the counterfeit note may not be in his own unaided powers, but in the light which his "detecter" gives him. That may, indeed, be so inscribed upon his memory, its light may be thus so transferred to his mind, that he will be able, at once, to indicate the forgery.

Christ is the Light of the world. He can scatter moral darkness, and easily expose all Satan's counterfeits, no matter how much angel-bleaching their surface may wear. Satan's disguises are nothing to his omniscient eye. The lies of Satan, whether black or white, are intended to misrepresent the character of God; but, of course, to Christ, it can not be successfully falsified; and when he reveals it, the world can know it as it is.

Our sure and only way, then, of triumph over the angel of false light, is to be so united to Christ by faith, so one with him in spirit and purpose, so acquainted with and wedded to him, that the light which is in him, and which he is, *will shine in our hearts*, enabling us to "behold him with open face," and, no less clearly, to see and detect the specious pretenses of Satan, transformed into his representative.

"Christ in you the hope of glory," Christ "the light of the world," is the grand New Testament moral and spiritual counterfeit detecter.

This real union of the soul to Christ, as its true Light and Life, is the great promise of the New Testament. It is symbolized in the union of the vine and branches, the head and the members. Paul prays for it when he bows his knee in behalf of the Ephesian Christians, and asks that Christ may dwell (Greek — dwell permanently) in their hearts. Jesus himself prays for it, when he asks the Father that his disciples "may be one in us," "I in them and thou in me," declaring that the glory which the Father had given him he had given them; and this grace is pledged to our faith in that great central promise of the New Testament, of the Holy Spirit to abide with us forever as our guide, teacher, and sanctifier. It is the very gist of the New Covenant and its "better promises," which guarantee the writing of God's law effectually upon the heart of the believer.

To have Christ, therefore, and his Spirit dwelling "with" and "in us," is to have within us a light which shall reveal to us the fictions, and forgeries, and false lights of Satan, and deliver us from their power.

The best illustration of this matter is found in the relation of two devoted hearts in perfect sympathy with each other, as those of husband and wife are supposed to be. Let such a husband undertake the overthrow of some huge system of iniquity which the influential and wealthy are selfishly interested to sustain, thus incurring their inevitable hatred and opposition. He goes on to expose the enormity of its wickedness, and the corrupt motives of those who uphold it; to show its injustice, its impolicy, its ruinous consequences, and to demand its destruction. The interested parties, of course, will resist; they will misjudge and misrepresent the reformer at every step, denouncing his motives as corrupt, and his spirit as malicious. They will play the angel of light to their system, and claim that it is scriptural, just, and humane; that their rights in it are sacred; that they are injured, and persecuted, and entitled to the sympathy of their fellow-men, while their opponent is worthy of death.

Now, persons watching the conflict, and having no acquaintance with the assailant, and being ignorant of the real merits of the case, might grossly misjudge him, and deem him a fanatic or a madman. But not so with that wife who occupies the same stand-point, who knows the reformer perfectly, and is in real sympathy with him. To her, he is all revealed, and the light of his character, shining in her, makes all clear, both on the side of the assailant and the assailed. That light, to her, perfectly refutes all the slanders against her husband, and holds her mind at perfect rest in a growing admiration of his character and confidence in his success. To know his will is easy, for her own is one with it. Knowing her husband as she does, how impossible it must be for his chief opponent so to transform himself into his character, as to be able to pass himself off to her in his stead!

Precisely so with the Christian who has found Christ as the indwelling light, and the bridegroom of the soul. The believer finds a beauty, a glory, an excellency in Jesus which can not be counterfeited. There is such a divine sweetness and fullness in his love, such a tenderness in his sympathy, such long-suffering in his patience, such life, even, in his smile, such satisfaction in his friendship, as can come from no finite mind. In his light, we have no need to be ignorant of Satanic devices. Satan might easily lead away a Judas with his false light, but could he thus deceive a John, a Paul, a Luther, or an Edwards?

5. Let there be a conscious dependence upon the Holy Spirit for light and guidance. It is his special mission to reveal Christ unto us. Be not afraid to follow the Spirit. He sheds light upon the reason. He does not impel his followers by blind impulses which bid defiance to common sense, but sweetly assures the heart, illumines the path, and shows it to be of God.

6. Do not commit the mistake of supposing that you can know all truth at once, but, in a submissive spirit, wait patiently for the light. Be willing to know a little, and then to grow in knowledge as fast as you can by a diligent use of means. You do not, at once, tell your child all you would have him know.

Do not condemn yourself that your attainments are so small, but only hunger and thirst after righteousness. Walk according to the light you have, and you can not fail to gain more. The Savior told the lepers to go and show themselves to the priest, and, *as they went*, they were healed. Be the little child, and lean not to your own understanding, and you shall be taught of God, and see light in his light.

7. Use the Bible as a detecter. I know Satan uses the Word, but not honestly. Compare the suspected truth with the tests which Christ presents, and observe all the marks. Put the doubtful sentiment under a magnifier. This is a quick way to expose

the counterfeit. A strong lens will at once show the difference between the genuine and the false note. In like way, take the moral counterfeit and look at it through the Sermon on the Mount, or through the cross, or through the life and spirit of Jesus, and its quality will soon be apparent.

8. Carry the suspected matter to God in prayer. If you present a package of notes to an expert cashier, his practiced eye will instantly detect the counterfeits. There is one in heaven whose eye can not be deceived.

9. Hold fast by faith, in an honest and truthful heart, to the promise of light from above. If thine eye be single, thy whole body shall be full of light. If any man lack wisdom, let him ask of God, who giveth to all men liberally, and it shall be given him. Following these instructions, the path shall grow brighter and brighter unto the perfect day.

10. Be humble. "God resisteth the proud, but giveth grace unto the humble." One of the seven sages, being asked what God had done, answered thus: "He has exalted humble men, and suppressed proud, ignorant souls." The lowly spirit is like the violet, which rises but a little way from the ground, hangs its head downward, hides itself in its own leaves, and is revealed by its fragrance.

CHAPTER XXI.

SATANIC PLOTS.—PASTOR'S SKETCH.

Lest Satan should get an advantage of us: for we are not ignorant of his devices.—2 *Cor.* 2 : 11.

THE great Captains of the world have gained their renown, very much, through the skillful and well-laid plans by which they have been able to circumvent, disappoint, and outwit their antagonists. With superior strategic ability, the commander of a small army will often destroy an enemy much stronger in numbers, in position, and in equipage.

Satan is a great strategist. He abounds in devices, and snares, and plots, wherewith to gain advantages over men for their moral destruction. His plans run back into early life, and include the putting of a lie upon the tongue of infancy, if possible, at its first utterance. They are often interwoven with our whole history. They may be slowly and cautiously developed, involved partly in one habit and partly in another. They may be designed to hedge up the sinner's way to the mercy-seat, or to confirm the soul in a state of skepticism and impenitence.

As an illustration of Satanic plots, I present the following

Pastor's Sketch.

Several years ago, the writer was laboring with a neighboring pastor, during a season of revival. "What shall we do to be saved?" was the one topic of inquiry in the community. One man, Mr. B., was so penetrated with the subject that he had no rest, night or day. With the pastor, I went to his house. A few moments' conversation revealed the fact that the Spirit was, indeed, striving with him. He seemed ripe for the acceptance of Christ as his Savior, and this act was urged upon him; to which he deliberately replied, "I shall never be a Christian." "Never be a Christian! Why not?" His only reply was, "I can not; it is impossible." "It is *not* impossible, God himself being witness, unless you have blasphemed the Holy Ghost: do you believe you have done that?" "I never meant to do it, and do not think I have." "Then your conclusion that you can not be a Christian is false; you can be; God invites you; the atonement is sufficient, though all the righteous blood shed upon the earth from that of Abel, were upon your soul; come and take the easy yoke of Christ." "Well, I can not help it; I shall never be a Christian." "But do you not wish to be one? Have you chosen to make your bed in hell? Have you found some fault with Christ, that you will not have him to reign over you?" "O, no, no; I do not *wish* to remain the enemy of one who has laid down his life to redeem me. Christ is all right; but it is of no use; I shall never be a Christian." "Sir, what is this which you have covered up in your heart, and which drives you to this terrible conclusion? There must be something there — something, no doubt, by which Satan means to destroy your soul." "I shall not tell you what it is." "But your salvation may depend upon your revealing it. Will you not retire and tell me in confidence?" "No, sir; I shall never reveal it." Turning to his wife, I asked, "Madam, do you know what this thing is?" "I do." "Will it do any harm for him to reveal it?" "Not the least, I think." Again turning to Mr. B., I said, "My dear sir, you *must* uncover this matter. Satan will drag you down to death and hell with this invisible halter. Come, out with it, and God will set you free." He shook his head negatively. I then told him the story of Father Carpenter and the New Jersey lady, given in a previous chapter, in order to show him the necessity and advantage of yielding to my entreaty. His only reply was, "I'll board you till you die, rather than tell you." It seemed impossible to move him; but God's Spirit was there, and we were not to be foiled. At length Mr. B. began to make suppositions. "Suppose a man has bound himself by a solemn oath never to do a certain thing; how is he ever to perform that thing?" "If the thing he swore not to do was a *right thing*, his oath does not and can not bind him. Were the men who swore they would kill Paul bound to do it? There is no such thing possible as a moral obligation to do what is wrong. The thing to be done, then, in respect to such an oath, is to repent of it, and break it as soon as possible." Even Satan could not successfully dispute this position, and it evidently made its impression. Then he said again, "Suppose a man had confessed himself guilty of a crime, and afterward, becoming a Christian, should deny the truth of his former confession; who *could* have any confidence in him that he was a Christian — could you?" "Peculiar case, surely. Men are not apt, when receiving forgiveness of sins, to justify themselves in conduct which they confessed criminal before they found mercy. A converted man would naturally intensify his confession of former transgressions. But, if I could see *the reason* why a man acknowledged guilt which did not belong to him, his withdrawal of the acknowledgment after his conversion would not, in the least, impair my confidence in him; for this would be his duty if he were not guilty.

"Now Mr. B., I suspect you. Do not these suppositions point to your difficulty?" "Well, I can not deny it." "*Very well; this dumb spirit must be cast out.* God forbid that Satan should cheat you out of eternal life in this way. What is the trouble?" But he was dumb still.

At this point, his pastor, Rev. Mr. C., deliberately said, "Mr. B., do you know that I am acquainted with this whole affair?" "No, sir! Are you?" "I am. My neighbor, Mr. W., has told me all." "*Mr. W. told you — did he?* Yes, I know him; he is my enemy." "But," said the good pastor, "be not offended with Mr. W.; he is your friend, not your enemy. He told me only for your good. He believes the adversary is making use of the affair to destroy your soul, and he wished me to know it, that I might help you to escape from the snare of the fowler: he loves you, and prays for you." The snare was broken. I said to him, "Sir, this is your hour; the waters in the pool are troubled; step in, and be made whole; kneel with us before the Lord, and let your heart offer the publican's prayer, God, be merciful to me a sinner." He was on his knees before the words had all fallen from my lips, with his heart broken and dissolved in tears. We prayed, while the wind of the Spirit blew upon him, and he arose evidently a new creature in Christ Jesus.

The facts in the case were these. When Mr. B. was a young man, some base fellows robbed a store of thirty dollars. They made a tool of him, and put the money into his hands, and told him to hide it, and he should have a part of it. In the thoughtlessness of his youth, he did as they told him. The next day, the robbery was discovered, and the lad betrayed himself by his fear and consternation. He was threatened with state prison, but was finally told, if he would confess and restore the money, nothing more should be done. He did so. The people understood, from his confession, that he was the original and only guilty party, whereas he knew he was not. He had suffered much from the affair; and, feeling that certain Christians, among whom was his then neighbor, Mr. W., had treated him unkindly, he had been led to take his oath that he would never be a Christian. It was a very natural difficulty which Satan now suggested, that, should he deny his former confession, he could never have the confidence of Christians as a fellow-disciple, and that it would, therefore, be in vain to attempt to become a Christian.

I had learned a new lesson touching the plots of Satan. After returning to my home in M., I prepared a sermon from the text at the head of this chapter, including in it the foregoing sketch. Having occasion, soon after, to preach for the Welsh church in the city, I used this discourse. On the next morning, there came to my door a fine-looking young foreigner, inquiring for the minister who had preached the night before at the Welsh church. From his broken speech, I learned that he had been greatly afflicted by the loss of his property and his friends; that he had been sorely disappointed in his mission to this country, so that he knew not which way to turn; that he felt that Satan had insnared him, so that his hope was well nigh extinguished, while he felt himself overwhelmed in the deep waters; and that he wished to give me many thanks; that, through my sermon, Jesus had "seized him by the hair of his head as he was sinking for the last time, and lifted him up, and set his feet again on the Rock of Ages."

It is hoped that the sketch above given may be of practical service to others.

The plots of Satan are numberless. He often, no doubt, pushes men into the commission of some disgraceful form of sin, foreseeing that, in all probability, they will never confess it and obtain pardon. Suppose a man, who has prided himself upon his reputation for honor and veracity in the community, suddenly finds his business affairs in such a state that failure stares him in the face. He sees but one way of escape. If his property would only take fire and burn up, the insurance money would save him. Satan suggests, — he meditates; — he can fire the premises, — his known integrity will shield him from suspicion. His heart beats quick; he must do it or fail; he yields, applies the torch, and his property is in ashes. He receives the insurance, and escapes failure. The man of honor is an incendiary, a thief, a liar, and a swindler, perhaps a murderer! and still he claims to be an honest man. What a snare! Will he ever escape from it? Will he ever confess his crime, and restore the money, that his sin may be blotted out? He may, but how fearfully *probable* that he will never do it!

Thousands, doubtless, are taken by some such

artful device of the adversary. Crimes lie buried in their hearts, while, peradventure, false names are assumed. Falsehood upon falsehood covers them, and, probably, nothing but the judgment of the great day, the rays of which will penetrate the darkest minds and reveal them as in sun-light, will ever disclose them. Such persons *are* "ignorant of Satan's devices."

Many of the principles of the business world, and of the customs and fashions of society, are used by a plotting adversary to draw men fatally away from their allegiance to Christ. With many, it is a settled principle, that real honesty and success in business are incompatible with each other. Surely a devotee of fashion can not be a follower of Jesus, the "meek and lowly." Let every man scrutinize the business and social maxims and customs by which he is governed, lest they involve some falsehood or some plot of the Devil designed to insnare and corrupt the soul!

There is, for most people, no influence in the world so strong as that which one living mind exerts over another. Recognizing this fact, Satan constructs many of his plots with reference to bringing the yet youthful and unsophisticated under the dominion of those who are advanced and established in vicious principles and habits. Wicked men, whom the adversary controls, are but the instruments wherewith he leads other men "captive at his will." And if he can take advantage of the example of a professedly good man, and so, the more unsuspected, fasten his halter to the neck of his victim, the more certainly will Satan make his plot succeed. Every one for himself, every parent for his child, every Christian for his fellow-disciple, should, therefore, watch ceaselessly against the mental and moral influence of evil-minded persons.

CHAPTER XXII.

SATAN THE ENEMY OF PRAYER AND VITAL COMMUNION WITH GOD.

Put on the whole armor of God, that ye may be able to stand against the wiles of the devil. Praying always with all prayer and supplication in the Spirit. — *Eph.* 6 : 11, 18.

An all-prevailing, unremitting spirit of prayer is an essential part of the Christian's invincible armor.

There is no truth more clearly set forth in the Bible than that God accepts and answers prayer. He has so pledged himself to do it, that he can not fail and be a God of truth. "Ask and it shall be given you," is the broad, unqualified promise. From Genesis to Revelation, assurance follows assurance, that the "eyes of the Lord are upon the righteous, and his ears open unto their cry." The fullness and positiveness of the promises only show how strongly God desires to have men approach his mercy-seat with loving boldness and humble confidence. Prayer is the connecting link between earth and heaven. It is the apparatus with which the soul draws its living waters from the deep wells of salvation. Communion with God is to the life of the soul what food is to the life of the body. The intensity of God's wish to save men from sin and death exactly measures his desire to bring them into communion with himself, by all possible means, but especially by prayer; for it is only by such heavenly intercourse, the soul can be lifted out of its sinfulness into the higher life of truth. Prayer ought to be as natural and easy, as full of confidence and affection, as free and joyous as the fellowship and converse of the most loving hearts. God would thus reveal himself to his people, and make them acquainted with his holy hatred of sin not only, but with his heart of yearning tenderness toward all the beings he has created, and with his peculiar love to his redeemed children; and so give them the light he would have them reflect upon the world. Men will know God, and be able to represent him truly, in proportion as their communion with him is intimate and habitual. The Bible will be luminous and life-giving, in the measure in which it is read and studied in the light of this heavenly intercourse. The providences of God will become significant and precious to the soul by the same rule. The spirituality of the law and the power of the gospel, the reality of God's attributes, character, and government, of heaven and of hell, of all our privileges here and our inheritance hereafter, will be seen and felt most deeply at the mercy-seat.

These things being obviously so, Satan will, of course, as one of his primary measures of evil, do his utmost to prevent our communion with God. He hates the closet and the throne of grace as he does Calvary and atoning blood. His opposition is not to all that is called prayer, but simply to that which involves the soul's vital approach to God. He is willing enough that men should multiply forms of prayer, and count their beads, and petition Allah at the Muezzin's call; and that the monks in the monastery of "The Conquering Angel" should pray night and day, forever, for the conversion of England to the Roman Catholic faith, and for whatever else may conflict with the will of God. Nay, he may be quite willing to facilitate all manner of praying which comes short of real communion with God.

What young convert, what Christian, does not Satan resist, "in coming to the mercy-seat"! From how many hearts, in the church even, has he quite obliterated the idea that such intimate communion with God as the promises imply, is possible! How many has he seduced into the notion, that God will not be influenced by our supplications, since he determined all his acts from eternity, — as if he did not, from eternity, foresee every true prayer that should ever be offered to him, and determine to answer it, — and that the only good of prayer is that which is to be gained by the exercise of offering it! To how many hearts has Satan suggested, "God will not hear *your* prayer;" "You are unworthy to commune with God — approach him not;" "You have sinned, and God will not hear you;" "You *can not* pray — it is *mockery* to attempt it;" and has thus repelled them from the mercy-seat! With such an incrustation of lies upon the sensibility, and while the mind remains in unbelief as to God's presence, and readiness to hear his people, of course prayer can not attain its natural expression, and is an unsatisfying service. To promote such unbelief Satan spares no pains.

The great remedy for all this mischief is to "resist the devil," and give God glory by believing and insisting that he *will* answer prayer honestly and truthfully offered according to his will. Some things, we know, are according to his will, and we may believe and ask for them, nothing doubting, as, for example, grace to honor God, strength to obey his word, wisdom to direct us, the gift of the Spirit to abide with and teach us the way of duty.

The religious world is full of facts illustrating the "power of prayer," and showing how it is answered. These anecdotes are valuable because instructive. Let us add the following : —

I once asked an intelligent parishioner this question : "Did you ever get cornered in your business, and prove the availability of prayer?" He smiled affirmatively, and said, "I was, at one time, on the verge of failure. A large amount of bank paper was maturing, and my resources for meeting it had entirely failed. I tried my best to provide means of payment, but to no purpose. There was but one more banker to whom I could go. To him I carried the whole case on my knees. I told him *I was willing to fail*, if, in his providence, he would have it so. But, if it could more honor my Savior that I should pay my debts, as a Christian man should do, I besought him to send me relief. I waited the result, believing God had heard my prayer. The consequence was, that, as my paper became due, men came to me, voluntarily, with just the amount I needed, asking me to take it, and pay them interest for the use of it. I was saved from failure; and I have had no trouble in paying my debts since that day."

Here is a fact showing that God has some peculiar ways of answering his children. That good brother Raymond, who went to Africa with the Amistad captives, and commenced the Mendi mission, and who has since gone to his rest, told me that, while he was preaching to the poor fugitives in Canada, who were scarcely able to give him his bread for his labor, he wore out his coat, and had no means of getting another. There was a brother with him who was also in want of five dollars. They concluded to carry their necessities to God, on retiring to rest on a bright moon-light night. Mr. Raymond told the Lord that his coat was very poor, threadbare, out at various places, and he did not think it was fit to preach so glorious a gospel in, and asked his Heavenly Father to help him to a new one. The other brother told the Lord, also, the story of his wants. In the course of the night, a wolf came about the house, whose howl awoke the young men. They arose, took their gun, and went out, and shot the wolf; and the bounty on it got the one a coat and the other five dollars. They believed in a "particular providence," and that God could turn the tables on the wolves, and make them feed the sheep.

In this connection, we think it may be of service to repeat a story which went the rounds of the papers some years ago.

As we remember it, certain clergymen had been disputing about the meaning of the command to "pray without ceasing." A plain, pious woman, meeting one of them, said, "I know what that passage means." She was invited to give her views, which she did by telling her experience, as follows: "When I rise in the morning, the first thing I do is to put on my clothes; and I pray God to clothe me with the robe of my Redeemer's righteousness, and with the garment of humility. The next thing I do is to build a fire; and I pray God to kindle the fire of love in my heart, that his word may be as a fire in my bones, and that I may escape the burning lake. The next thing I do is to sweep the floor; and I pray that Jesus will sweep from my heart all the dirt and dust which his eye sees there. Then I set the table; and I pray that I may sit at the marriage supper of the Lamb, and be bountifully supplied with the bread of life. If I sit, I pray that I may sit at the feet of Jesus;

if I stand, that it may be in his righteousness, and upon the Rock of Ages; if I walk, that it may be with God, like Enoch; if I run, that I may run the race with patience, and safely reach the goal."

Thus this mother in Israel showed how, in her state of mind, every thing about her suggested a topic of prayer, and kept her spontaneously communing with God. Was ever a passage of Scripture better expounded?

Every Christian may make his " calling and election sure" by maintaining, inviolate, habitual communion with God.

The devices of Satan to break up the soul's communion with God are numerous and subtle.

If a man *will go* to his closet, the adversary will, if possible, seduce him into a practical unbelief as to the presence, there, of Christ, and into a mere formal service, in which he will have no real intercourse with God, and which will only foster the spirit of self-righteousness, or be suggestive of doubts and fears.

Satan would have men think the mercy-seat inaccessible, or induce the feeling that it is located in some uninviting Terra del Fuego, where the weather never clears, instead of a Buenos Ayres, where the atmosphere is always balmy and beautiful. He would have men believe that the throne of grace can be approached only by the pure and holy; whereas it was established expressly, and located " not far from every one of us," that the unworthy, the helpless, the sinful might find succor. He takes advantage of our relapses and failures to repel us from its approach; whereas they constitute the strongest reasons for frequenting that refuge for lost sinners. Herein Satan utterly misrepresents our Heavenly Father. The Good Shepherd is specially regardful of the weak and erring. Would that all understood this as well as did Peter! A sheep may fall into the ditch, and be a sheep still—widely different from the swine whose instincts all incline him to go there.

Satan, moreover, brings his own will to bear directly against that of the disciple, to keep him from drawing near to God by prayer. Minds seem constituted to resist as well as to help each other. When a father sets his will against that of his child, forbidding him to do a given thing, a real force is put into operation. When the public will is set in a particular direction, it is difficult to resist and overcome it. It is like a moral avalanche. This resistance belongs to the *will* of the masses, rather than to mere "public sentiment," as the phrase is. A sentiment which has not entered into the *voluntary life* of the people, has slight moral power. The creed of a church weighs little until it is incorporated into their practice. Our national doctrine of liberty is powerless for good, while we *willingly* agree to hold men in bondage. This vast will-power, his own and that which inheres in the example of the prayerless multitude, Satan throws across the pathway of the Christian, especially as it leads to the mercy-seat, forbidding his advance in that direction. To break from this restraining influence, especially when it emanates from intimate associates and kindred, from men of mark and wealth, and from that sex whose will often has the force of social law, is, to the young and inexperienced in religion, no easy matter. But, taking advantage of the help there is in the inspiring will of the "great cloud of witnesses" above, in the example of the Jacobs and Elijahs, and the hosts of royal men around us who live by communion with the Holy One, in the name of the Omnipotent, we can and should overcome all obstacles, and live in habitual and blessed intercourse with our God and Savior.

Muller's "Life of Trust" has raised the question, whether we may expect the prayer of faith to be answered, independently of the use of means on the part of the suppliant. That servant of God professes to have received the funds necessary to carry forward his charitable work, soliciting them from no man, but from God only. A few words on this subject, in this connection, as guarding against any error of which Satan might take advantage, may not be out of place.

The Bible, as well as reason, proves that God has established the connection between means and ends, and required men to use their own agency, as far as they may, in supplying their wants. In addition to this, the help of God is indispensable; and for this we are to pray. The Bible teaches that Divine and human agency are united in the production of results. "*That thou givest them they gather*," says the Psalmist (104 : 28). In many of the miracles, even, secondary agency was introduced, as in that of furnishing wine at the marriage in Cana, of feeding the multitudes, and of opening the eyes of the blind. The answer to prayer may be as legitimate and palpable in supplying us with the *means* of gaining the blessing we seek, as in bestowing directly the object for which we pray. This is strikingly illustrated by the case of the two brethren and the wolf, just narrated. There are cases, indeed, where it would be impossible to employ any subordinate instrumentalities, as where Elijah, on Carmel, prays for rain. He could only pray and *watch*. In such cases, of course, the use of means is not required.

There is nothing in the experience of the author of the "Life of Trust" which goes to impair the old Christian doctrine on this subject, that the suppliant must pray, and watch, and *work* by all legitimate methods, in order that his prayers may be answered.

Mr. Muller himself, after all, acted upon this principle. The means he used were peculiar, but potent. He really asked every Christian man to aid him in building his orphan houses, when he made known the fact, or when it became known, that he was building them in the name of the Lord, and for the use of

God's poor and helpless ones, and that he was trusting the Lord alone to supply the funds. By this very position, mutely but loudly, he said to every man, "This is purely a Christian work; it is a privilege to promote it; how can you withhold your gifts from such an enterprise?" And in proportion as confidence was felt in the principles of the Bible, and in Mr. Muller as a true and wise servant of God, contributions did, naturally enough, by the grace of God, and in answer to prayer, flow into his hands. He could scarcely have plied the minds of good men more effectually with motives to benevolence. He exercised a trust which, under the circumstances, God was pleased greatly to honor. But was the hand of the Lord less visible in providing the means for building the temple, when David himself offered, as some reckon, over 50,000,000 pounds sterling, and then called upon the people to follow his example, and bring in their offerings, which they did with a similar liberality? With glad and joyous hearts they acknowledged that all they had was the Lord's, and that it was by his grace that they had been enabled to offer so willingly and abundantly unto him. Was it not an additional blessing to David, and to the people, that God was pleased to answer his prayer for means, by making his own appeal to his subjects effectual? In other words, is there not a substantial good in having our own agency employed in the work of answering our prayers; and should we not, therefore, expect God so to employ it?

We must not forget that it is the "effectual fervent prayer of a righteous man" which "availeth much;" nor should we overlook the necessity of importunity, as enjoined by Christ in the parable of the unjust judge. It is not, indeed, to be supposed that God requires the urgency there inculcated, for its own sake, as if he needed something to excite his benevolence. It is demanded rather in accordance with that law of our being by which we put forth our intensest efforts to obtain that which we most highly prize. If we value spiritual blessings as we should, we shall naturally act according to the spirit of that parable, and, like Jacob, refuse to let the Angel of the Covenant go, except he bless us.

If Satan can not wholly prevent our intercourse with God, he will try to silence our importunity, lest we should obtain the higher and richer blessings of the kingdom, and be effectually avenged of him as the enemy of our souls.

There is no more precious truth in connection with this subject, than that our ever-living Intercessor by virtue of his own sacrifice, presents for us, at the throne of God, the supplications which the Spirit, helping our infirmities, has begotten in us, and which our faith importunately urges, and, that he is sure to prevail. Against that intercession, Satan is powerless.

CHAPTER XXIII.

SATAN AS PHILOSOPHER, THEOLOGIAN, AND LOGICIAN.

Oppositions of science, falsely so called; which some, professing, have erred from the faith.—1 *Tim.* 6: 20.

THE roots of our theology penetrate and draw their life from our underlying philosophy; so that, if our mental science be false, our theological system can not be true, and we "err from the faith" by inevitable necessity. Our philosophy must determine all our essential definitions in theology, and furnish us our laws for interpreting the word, the character, and the government of God. It will, consciously or unconsciously, shape our experiences, and stamp itself effectually upon our lives.

All this Satan knows full well, for he is an old and careful student of the nature and laws of mind. He will see to it, therefore, that, as far as possible, our mental and moral science shall be only "falsely so called," that he may subvert the very foundations on which the structure of objective truth must rest. He is to be regarded as the father of scientific lies, not less than others, but rather more so, if he can connect with them more disastrous consequences. He is doubtless the father, too, of that popular notion that teachers of religion should ignore the subject of mental philosophy as altogether unprofitable. He would be glad to be let alone in the work of constructing the molds by which our religious systems, and creeds, and habits must be shaped.

Let us attempt to expose Satan as a false philosopher and theologian, in respect to a few important topics.

1. The doctrine of the will is cardinal in its relations to theology. There are two theories concerning its nature. One is, that it is free in its choices; that the choice is of the man himself, and is, therefore, what he determines it to be. The other is, that the choice is the necessary and unavoidable result of the motives before the mind; so that it is not determined at all by the man himself. A person deliberately commits a murder that he may possess himself of his victim's gold. The gold is the motive to the act of murder. If there had been no gold, there would have been no motive to the crime, and it would not have been committed. But the motive existed; it was before the mind, and appealed to the murderer to do the desperate deed. Now, on the theory of freedom in the will, it is maintained that the man had the power, in his nature, to resist the wrong motive and obey the right one — to choose between the opposing motives, and determine whether to commit the crime, or remain an innocent man. That he did

yield, and commit the crime, is, therefore, held to be his own guilty act, for which he is justly responsible. The motive was the occasion; the reason, why he acted; the actor was himself. On the theory of necessity, on the other hand, it is held, that the relation between the motive and the volition which took the life, was such, that the act or crime of murder could not have been avoided. The motive, not the man, was the real murderer, as the fire is the real cause of the boiling of the water.

That the former is the true doctrine, we have sufficiently shown in Chapter IV. The latter theory we regard as "science falsely so called," and full of deadly error.

Christian philosophers who adopt the false theory are prevented, by their piety and by the Scriptures, from seeing and acknowledging all its baleful deductions. But atheistic and rationalistic philosophers leap at once from such premises to the denial of Christianity, and of the divine existence, and of any real distinctions in character and morals.

In proportion as men practically adopt this error, — and many do adopt it in religion, as Satan would have them, though never in regard to the affairs of this life, — the following, among other evil consequences, will follow: there will be no sense of obligation, actively and earnestly, and at all times, to obey God; for we are so made that we *can not* feel obligation to what we believe we have no power, in our natures, to do.

The mind will be thrown into a passive state, and be shorn of its strength. The soul can make no stand against the forces of evil, and must drift passively with them — the mere creature, and not the creator of events, the slave, and not the master of circumstances. The soul is not even an agent; it is a mere vessel through which the waters are at liberty to flow.

Faith can be little more than a name — a dead profession; for the vital element of that grace, on the human side of it, is the voluntary one — the will, consciously grasping the truth, by the grace of God, and making its power the soul's own. "All things are possible to him that believeth," is true, because he chooses the object of faith, and *determines* to do the bidding of faith; but if a man denies his power thus to will, he denies that which is essential to the life and vigor of his faith; and, instead of being able to do all that a believer ought to do, he will do nothing, and will become the easy prey of Satan.

All the Christian graces are, by this false theory, impaired, to say the least. For what can love, self-denial, gratitude, or repentance amount to, if they have not in them the element of *conscious choice* and determination? When a man is full of determined energy and devotion toward God, toward right and truth, — when self-will is renounced, and Christ is supremely chosen and enthroned in his heart, — he becomes a power in the world to influence and control men, to overcome obstacles, and to mold society; he is like Paul, a living demonstration of the truth of Christianity; but the man who adopts the false theory slumbers in his passivity. With this philosophy, the doctrine of dependence naturally becomes perverted. Its advocates are likely to depend hopelessly upon God for an ability they already possess, and do not recognize, instead of depending, as they should, for that fuller, clearer, and higher knowledge of himself by which we are to grow into his moral likeness, and more and more completely and efficiently execute his will.

Under the influence of this mistaken theory, our view of sin is, of course, most injuriously confused and distorted. Instead of a stubborn refusal to use our voluntary powers as God, for the best of reasons, requires, — a most wicked rebellion against his authority and contempt of his mercy, — sin comes to be viewed as something so connected with our very natures, that we can scarcely know what it is, or see any guilt in it, or how to escape it, or why we are condemned for it, or called upon to repent of it. Then, as a natural result of this false and indefinite notion, the whole gospel, as a means of saving us from sin, is necessarily involved in the same confusion and indefiniteness. If a man steals his neighbor's property, his soul is stung with condemnation; he sees and knows his guilt; but, lulled by this most delusive speculation, men live in the constant violation of God's laws without a blush upon their cheeks.

It is, therefore, another consequence of this false theory, that it becomes next to impossible to convict men of sin before God. Our sanctuaries are full of persons who are unmoved by any appeals to repent of sin; and the reason is, that they have adopted Satan's great scientific falsehood, and said, with the Jews, "If our sins and our iniquities be upon us, how should we then live?" "We can not help ourselves."

Thanks be to God, and to the deep consciousness of our freedom, men can not act, in all respects, as if they were mere machines, nor rest in blank atheism, as they would otherwise be led to do. This error, however, is one of the very strongest of the adversary's intrenchments, and is the ultimate basis of nearly all the forms of infidelity, from universalism to atheism, inclusive. None of them can stand a moment in argument, only as they fall back upon this philosophy, "falsely so called."

2. Another of the leading and most bewitching of the false principles of Satanic mental philosophy, is the doctrine that we are to judge ourselves by our emotional experiences, rather than by our conscious *voluntary* conformity, or want of conformity, to the truth and will of God.

We have before said that Satan attacks the mind,

mainly, through the sensibility. The law of God being written upon the reason, his assault upon that power directly would be less likely to succeed. He must somehow make darkness appear to be light, and light, darkness; and this he can easily accomplish, if he can induce men to accept *a state of the emotions as the practical standard of right.*

This is precisely what Satan does: he "puts it into men's hearts" that they are *right* when they are the subjects of a certain state of religious feeling, and *wrong* when they are not. If *that* exists, they suppose they have faith and love, and are, therefore, accepted of God; if that does not exist, they conclude that God has rejected and will not hear them. They give up their confidence, quit the mercy-seat, "hang their harps on the willows," and go into a chronic despondency "by the cold streams of Babylon." It becomes the great, unnatural struggle of their religious life to gain and retain the peculiar state of the emotions which they have accepted as the standard of what is right and pleasing to God. Our churches abound with such mistaken souls. Their religion is at the mercy of the winds, rising or falling with the mercury in the sensibility.

The consequences of this error will be apparent to all who will reflect upon them.

The mind is intimately related to the body, and our emotions are often, unavoidably, as the state of bodily health. A wretched dyspeptic can scarcely *praise* the Lord, emotionally, if he tries ever so hard, though he may hold heroic fellowship with the sufferings of Christ.

Making our emotions the test and guide of our moral conduct, we ignore, of necessity, the guidance of our reason, whereon the divine image is enstamped, and in which his light shines. We must also fail to make the Word of God or the Spirit of God, our guide, unless, indeed, it happens to coincide with our feelings.

Another most lamentable consequence of this error will be, that we shall defeat the purpose of God in respect to our moral discipline and growth. These come by steadfastly obeying the truth, even when the sensibility is in a furnace heated to sevenfold intensity. The only way to stand with those "who have come up through great tribulation," is to be firm in patient adherence to the divine will, although the ocean of temptation and sorrow roll over us, as the waters sometimes sweep over the Eddystone lighthouse in the English Channel. This we can not do, if we make our feelings our standard of judgment.

Such a rule of duty also interferes, directly and ruinously, with the exercise of faith, and of all other Christian graces. The glory of Abraham's faith consisted in the fact that he persisted, with his whole voluntary power, in the faithfulness of God, although his sensibility was ready "to stagger" at the promise, whose fulfillment was so long delayed. To walk by faith is often to contradict sight. No man will ever be led, *by his feelings*, to the cross and the stake.

This philosophy overlooks the respective offices of the sensibility and of the reason, and almost interchanges them. All experience must harmonize with the true nature and laws of mind. Make the will of God, as expressed in the Bible, and re-affirmed in the reason, the standard of duty; do it, though temptation clamor never so much against it; and, in due time, the sensibility will fulfill its own office, and give you the very peace of God which passes all understanding. "Ye have need of patience, that, after ye have done the will of God, ye may receive the promise." Following the false science of the enemy, you are, on the other hand, at sea without helm, chart, or compass.

A true philosophy, leaving the *sensibility* essentially to its own organic laws, bids the soul lay hold of the truth of God as its life, to sink or swim with that, to anchor to it, though the waters roar and be troubled, and the mountains shake with the swelling thereof; and it charges the eye of consciousness to watch, not the state of the emotions, but of the will, to see that it does, not in word only, but in deed, so stand and risk all upon the truth. Thus fortified, the soul spreads to the breeze her pennant, inscribed with "Emanuel," and fears not to clear the shore and make for mid-ocean. If the sensibility rocks to the winds, rises and falls with the tides, or drifts with the currents of the sea; if she is depressed as night darkens over and around her, and, anon, thrilled and exalted in the day's clear uprising, with joys "unspeakable and full of glory," as she sees God above and only God all around; or if, again, she be strained to utmost tension by the storms which beat upon her, — it matters not. All is well. Christ is in the ship, and, at the right moment, he will arise and say to the sea, "Peace, be still;" and there will be a great calm reaching the very depths of the soul.

3. Satan, as a false philosopher, does men immense mischief by leading them into a perverted use of the faculty of judgment. To misuse this important member of the mental confederacy, is to warp the action of the whole mind. When the Scribes and Pharisees *judged* that Christ was an impostor, they would not, of course, bow to his instructions; they must needs oppose him, and do their utmost to destroy his influence. This false judgment would discolor all he could do or say in their behalf. Even his miracles, in giving sight to the blind or hearing to the deaf, would only suggest to their minds that he was an agent of Satan. They could not thus love or revere him.

So, if a man has *judged* that he is not a sinner, as the Bible represents, he will not repent and believe the gospel. If one has *judged* that there is no mercy for him, as thousands have, it is certain he will not labor to obtain it. When the Christian *judges* that the grace of God is not sufficient for him, so that he can walk in the light and overcome the world, the certain result is, that he will walk in darkness down to his grave. His false judgment dooms him to this. If you deliberately decide, in your *judgment*, that the promises of God do not belong to you, that the provisions of grace are not for you, or that they are not available for you now, then, plainly, you have cast away a present gospel from your soul. This false judgment arrests, too, the work of your sanctification by the Spirit; for he works by sealing upon the heart the truths and promises of God. In short, such an attitude of mind as effectually hinders the saving influences of Christianity from doing us good, as the prejudice of the Pharisees destroyed the power of Christ to be a Savior to them. In this way, the gospel, with all its fountains, and streams, and oceans of living water, is turned into a waste and desolate wilderness. Words can not describe the mischief which comes of thus perverting the office of the judgment. Let every one beware of Satan, by remembering *not* to judge according to appearances, not according to states of feeling, but according to God's testimony in his word, for this only is "righteous judgment." An honest and true use of this faculty of the mind is, on the other hand, above all price.

4. Satan aims to subordinate the *memory* to his purposes. This is one of the most important of our mental faculties, as, by it, the truth is to be treasured up and held for use. By the truth of God we are to be sanctified. But to be of much advantage to us, we must possess and hold it in the memory. Now, it is one law of the mind, that the memory will be deeply and permanently impressed in proportion to the wakefulness of the attention. But how easily is this turned off from the truths we hear or read, so that only a faint and ineffectual impression is made upon us! The game of Satan, therefore, is to divert the attention. This he will do, even in the house of God, by a multitude of suggestions, and at the very moment when the things most important to be remembered are uttered. If he can not wholly prevent a good and true impression, he will, if possible, warp it into something comparatively harmless to his ends. The method, then, by which Satan "catches away" the word sown in our hearts, and plants his own seeds of death there, is *by turning the attention from the truth, and by fixing it where the evil thought will fall most impressively upon the mind.* The thing to be done, on the other hand, is, not to let the attention swing loosely, like a weathercock in the wind, but, by a vigorous act of the will, hold it steadily and earnestly to the truth. It should be held there as the student holds his mind to the problem, as the judge, to the case before him, and as

the imperiled mariner, to the chances of relief. Let the mind be educated to it. Gain the power by persevering effort and rigid discipline; otherwise Satan will steal away all the good seed from the soul, and turn the mind itself into a sieve, instead of a vessel honored and meet for the Master's use.

5. It is a doctrine of Satanic philosophy, *that the testimony of our consciousness as to our moral and spiritual states can not be relied upon.* Admitting this, we must needs be in the greatest doubt and uncertainty respecting our personal relations to God. Our senses can, of course, give us no light; and, if we deny the validity of consciousness, as Satan would have us, there is no light for us. In the sphere of our experiences toward each other, the authority of consciousness is undisputed. By its witnessing, we *know* that we love our friends, that we confide in them, and that we are faithful or otherwise to the trusts committed to us; we *know* what are our intentions, and what our chosen aims.

By the same faculty of our minds, according to a true philosophy, we can *know* that we have chosen Christ as our portion, or that we have not done so; that we have, or have not, a real intention to conform to his will and please him in all our ways; that we do, or do not, really intrust ourselves to him for salvation, on the conditions of his gospel. Of course, we can not know our moral exercises as we know a mathematical demonstration, but we may so know them as to *satisfy* the mind, free it from *doubt*, and give it *rest* and *confidence*. So the wife knows her relations to her husband, the child, to the parent, and the friend, to the friend.

With the mind encumbered with this philosophy, "falsely so called," we are unavoidably deprived of the testimony of the Spirit. There is no power, but that of consciousness, through which the Holy Ghost can give his assurances to our hearts.

Thus does this false philosophy, so far as it is accepted as true, wither the life and cripple the power of Christian men. By it, the wings of God's eagles are clipped, and they can not fly; and the lambs of the flock are exposed to the wolf on every hand.

The intelligent reader will scarcely need to be told, that, while he is to hold fast the testimony of his own conscious purpose of obedience and trust, it is, of course, necessary to guard against the various delusions by which Satan himself would seek to deceive us in reference to our moral states. This is evermore to be done by appealing to the tests of God's word.

6. We may profitably consider here the philosophy by which Satan leads men "captive at his will."

We have certain appetites, desires, susceptibilities, which demand gratification. Besides the common bodily appetites, there is the desire for society, for reputation, for knowledge, for occupation; and the susceptibility which distinguishes us as male and female. These, and many others, God has implanted in our natures; and, in themselves, they are good. They are involuntary, and simply demand gratification without any reference to the question of right or wrong. The law which should regulate their gratification is not written upon the appetites themselves, and, therefore, men may involuntarily desire what they would have no right to appropriate. This regulating law is to be found rather in the *reason*, in the Bible, and in the lights of science.

It is the office of the *will*, in its God-given sovereignty, to give or withhold the gratification which the desires demand — if the drunkard's appetite clamors for the glass, to say in reply, "Yes, take the burning draught," or to answer, "No, not a drop;" and so it shall be.

Motives reach the will both through the appetites and the reason. Those which come through the former simply demand gratification because this is pleasurable. Those which come through the latter — the reason — bid the will to gratify the appetites according to the law of right.

Now, in this exigency, Satan brings the whole strength of his influence and his lies to bear upon the will to induce a decision to gratify the appetites and desires, in ways forbidden by the reason and the moral law. He will stimulate them to an unnatural importunity for indulgence; he will help men to conclude that natural desires may, of right, have the very gratification they call for, without reference to any higher rule; he will inflame the imagination, and set fire to the lusts of the flesh by a poisonous literature, and by all manner of appliances in art, in dress, in food, and in the customs of society, and thus, if he be allowed to do it, *carry the will*, and get it committed to the appetites rather than to the reason.

The issue, then, pending before the mind, is fearful beyond the power of the finite mind to comprehend. If it shall yield but once, and trample upon the law of reason, at the bidding of the tempter, the risk is terrible; if twice or thrice, "the letting out of waters" has begun; if, by a course of repetitions, the *habit* of yielding becomes fixed, the victim is in the cataract, hard upon the precipice and the terrible abyss below! In this way, the unregulated lusts of the lower nature gain the supremacy, and the will and reason break asunder. Then comes the most terrible of all calamities: God gives the victim up "to his own heart's lusts," and he is in the hands of the most merciless set of tyrants which earth or hell can furnish, — ambition, avarice, gluttony, sensuality, licentiousness, — and they assume the reins and drive whither they will. The restraints of reason are gone, and the soul is indeed "led captive by Satan at his will." Truth, with all her blessed angels, utterly banished, the mind is swept on "in the broad road to death" by a tornado of lies and lusts. The conscience becomes all seared with the hot iron of sin and shame; the imagination, no longer heaven-winged, is prone only to the earth; the intellect, sharing the common degradation, lives on divine thought no longer; the will expends its energies in gratifying fleshly appetites, when it should be creating blessings for a lost world, and opening fountains to send out living streams while the ages roll away. Especially, when a depraved sexual appetite gains the ascendency, natural affection, even, must soon die out; homes will be blasted; children will be made worse than orphans, for the sake of guilty fellowship with forbidden lovers.

This is a method of ruining souls, too, as Satan knows full well, by which his victims grow rapidly worse and worse, till they will glory in their shame, and take willingly, in their very foreheads, the seal of his kingdom and lordship.

The character of Satan as a logician demands a moment's notice. Man has reason, and he will use it. The father of lies must, therefore, work his falsehoods into logical forms, in order to make them hold with reasoning minds. "To make the worse appear the better reason," to shape falsehood so as to make it pass for truth under the rigid scrutiny of the logician, is a great feat of the adversary. Thousands of good men are captured by Satanic logic. Many reason vaguely thus: Major premise, God has made me; minor premise, God will take care of what he has made; conclusion, therefore, I shall be saved. The falsehood lurks in the major premise, because it does not contain the whole truth: God has made us *moral agents*, and we have something to do ourselves to secure our salvation. A majority of Universalists have probably been made such by the reasoning contained in the following syllogisms: It is the dictate of infinite love and mercy to save all mankind; God's love and mercy are infinite; he will save all mankind. Here, too, the lie is in the major premise, which assumes as true the very thing which demands proof, viz., that love and mercy dictate the salvation of all mankind, *unconditionally*. Again: God wishes the salvation of all men, as is manifest from his word and character; being infinite in wisdom and power, he will surely bring his wishes to pass; therefore, all men will be saved. Here the falsehood is in the minor premise. It is not true that God brings all his wishes to pass. He wishes men would not break his laws, and wrong and murder each other; yet he does not compel them to do his pleasure, but leaves them, as moral agents, to do their own will, and holds them answerable at his bar for their sins.

Again: impartiality is an attribute of God; impartiality requires that, if any are saved, all should be; therefore (since it is admitted that some will be), all must be saved. But the minor premise is a most absurd falsehood. Impartiality requires only that the offer of salvation, with its conditions, should be the same for all; and then, that all men should be treated exactly according to their characters.

The true argument from God's love stands thus: It is the dictate of infinite love and mercy to save every one that will comply with the just and indispensable conditions of salvation; God's love and mercy are infinite; therefore, he will save every one who repents of sin, believes the gospel, and submits to the divine authority; in other words, he will save all whom he consistently can save. Any larger inference than this from the love of God is totally false and illogical.

Again: it is unreasonable to suppose that the punishment of sin will be materially longer than the time required to commit it; sin is the work of a moment, or of a brief lifetime; therefore, its punishment will not be eternal. Falsehood lurks in both these premises. In the first place, there is no relation between the time required to commit the sin and its evil desert. All common sense forbids us to measure the guilt of firing a city by the moment of time required to do it.

But, moreover, sin in its essence, as distinguished from the external act, has the element of eternity in it, and is not the work of a moment, or of a brief lifetime, at all. Stealing is the determination to appropriate to yourself what belongs to another; and this for all time. It is the mind's settled and continued choice. It can never end except by repentance, confession, and conversion; and so the endless punishment of unrepented sin will only run parallel with the sin itself.

Again: modern skepticism reasons thus: God has a universal law of progress and development, from lower to higher, for all his creation capable of such advancement; man, of course, belongs to the creation, and is capable of progress; therefore, mankind will universally progress from the low state of sin to the complete purity and righteousness attainable in heaven. The Satanic element may be easily detected in this reasoning. We know of no law by which it is certain that all men must and will advance from sin to holiness. There is an utter destitution of evidence that any moral influences whatever can necessitate the development of men in virtue. Men, by their constitutions, are as capable of progressing in wickedness as in holiness; and they do progress in the direction of their supreme choices. All observation and experience, as well as Scripture, proves that "evil men and seducers wax worse and worse," and that they do often, under the best possible moral influences, harden and corrupt their moral natures.

Again: many are being led into grievous error by an argument which stands thus: the "death," the "destruction," the "perishing," or "burning up" of men, signifies the utter and endless extinction of their being; the Bible teaches and experience proves that the wicked will "die," be "destroyed," will "perish," and be "burned up ;" therefore, the wicked will be utterly annihilated. But the major premise is palpably false. No such meaning is given now, nor ever has been, in any part or age of the world, to the term *death*, or any of its synonyms. The continued existence of men after death has been the belief of the race from the earliest periods. It was the faith of the Egyptians before the days of Moses. The Hebrews held the same view. The continued existence of men in another life was so real to them, that a law, with the penalty of death, was required to prevent their substitution of the supposed counsels of the departed for the commandments of God.

But our chapter is sufficiently extended. We have said enough, perhaps, to put the reader on his guard against Satan as a philosopher, theologian, and logician.

CHAPTER XXIV.

THE ALLIES OF SATAN.

The devil and his angels.— Matt. 25 : 41.

IT is but natural to suppose that Satan will employ all the agents and instrumentalities he can, animate and inanimate, in this and other worlds, for the furtherance of his malign purposes. The Bible represents the fallen angels as his allies, and wicked men on the earth as his servants.

The brief consideration of a few important principles will help to make clear the subject of this chapter — the allies of Satan.

First, then, sin is a unit. The law of God, which it violates, demands but one thing. That can be expressed in one, ten, or ten thousand specific commandments. Christ summed it up in two precepts; Paul enunciated it by the one word, Love. That simple love which treats God as supreme in excellence, and in authority over us, and which practically regards the interests of our fellow-man as equal to our own, fulfills it. Each possible specific sin is but a transgression of this one principle.

Again: the *forms* of sin are *innumerable*. The

wrong state of the mind, which the moral law forbids, may, with equal facility, express itself in all sorts of wrong outward deeds; as, on the other hand, the right state of the mind, which the same law enjoins, may manifest itself by all the right acts which have ever been put forth on earth or in heaven.

Again: the radical state of mind in all transgressors, on earth or in hell, is the same, however numerous, or widely different, their outward acts of sin may be. There may be great constitutional differences among men, giving rise to endless varieties of outward development; there may, as in the case of the young ruler, be a natural beauty of character, vailing and seeming almost to overcome the deep-seated selfish greed within; or there may be the undisguised and repulsive accompaniments which marked a Herod and a Nero; and yet all may proceed from the same fountain of natural selfishness. The thief has his way of securing his selfish ends; the liar has his; and so have the moralist, the devotee of fashion, the amiable worldling, and every unregenerate man. This is clearly the doctrine of the Bible. "They are all gone aside, they are altogether become filthy; there is none that doeth good; no, not one" (Ps. 14: 12). "Whosoever shall keep the whole law [outwardly], and yet offend in one point, he is guilty of all" (James 2: 10), because his supremely selfish purpose or will, which deliberately breaks a single commandment, involves the violation, in spirit, of all moral precepts. This is the bitter fountain from which all transgression flows.

Again: all forms of sin are radically allied to, and in sympathy with each other. In a war of aristocracy against democracy, aristocrats, the world over, will be in sympathetic alliance with their warring brethren; for their own principles are involved in the struggle; and they will, as far as their local selfish interests will allow, build them iron-clads, loan them money, create favorable public sentiment, turn truth into lies and lies into truth to strengthen their hands and weaken their opponents, and do, in short, whatever they can to sustain their friends and keep the people down. It will even make little difference under what form of government they may live, or by what oaths and treaties they may be bound. And so, universally, all forms of sin and of virtue are, in the nature of the case, in intimate fellowship with each other.

Again: all sin is against God as the rightful Sovereign of the universe. And so identical in principle are the interests of all moral beings, that it is impossible to sin against one without sinning against all; and David could say to his Maker truly, "Against thee, thee only, have I sinned, and done this evil in thy sight;" and Jesus could declare, "Inasmuch as ye have done it unto one of the least of these my brethren, ye have done it unto me."

Again: the alliance between the Devil and his

angels is an alliance against God, and all beings over whose interests the moral law spreads its ægis — an alliance formed by the force of homogeneous principles, by the action of the natural impulse to fortify, strengthen, and protect ourselves, and by virtue of those laws of our being which spontaneously impel us to take part with those who are in fellowship and sympathy with us, in thought, feeling, and purpose. Chemical affinities are not more unvarying than are moral and spiritual ones. Our mental and spiritual states have an attracting and a repelling power, but faintly shadowed forth by those of the material world.

Again: whether Satan be an absolute sovereign in his dominions, or a representative one, elected by the parliament of hell, his subjects are all made such by their own free choice and preference. The alliance between them is, therefore, intimate and powerful. His servants are known, in the Bible, as his children. He is their father and their god. They trust in him; they adopt his principles; they obey and imitate him. They cleave to him, in spite of the remonstrances of reason and conscience, and the authority and infinite love of God. They credit his word rather than that of Him who can not lie. They serve their father with a zeal worthy of a better sonship, and that, while they know full well that they are trampling upon the blood of Christ, and exposing themselves to his eternal anathema. The alliance, indeed, is not formal, as between states, but, being a thing of life and of sympathetic gravitation, it is even more radical and effective.

If these principles are correct, it follows that every unregenerate sinner in the moral universe is in alliance with Satan. Supremely selfish men on earth are as really his allies as if they were in the spirit world doing his bidding. They do not perform the same service as his disembodied angels, but they build his theaters, they run his distilleries, they oppress the poor, they tempt the weak, they pervert justice, and, in the place of true religion, they do but make a "fair show in the flesh." Paul affirms that "the poison of asps is under their lips," that their "mouth is full of cursing and bitterness," that "their feet are swift to shed blood," and that "destruction and misery are in their ways." In that mightiest war known in the world, in which Satan leads his hosts against the Redeemer of mankind, to annihilate the principles which shone in his life, and which he sealed with his blood on Calvary, all the rejecters of Christ are the inflexible allies of his great enemy, the Devil. They will not have Christ to reign over them; they oppose him with the whole force of their example; they spurn the invitations of his love and mercy. The Bible clearly asserts the moral hostility of the unregenerate to Christ. They "hate him," and that, "without a cause." "The carnal mind is enmity against God." Representative men cried out against him, and said, "Crucify him, crucify him;" and then, that their cry might be heard, welcomed the guilt of the unparalleled crime, as the awful inheritance of themselves and their children forever (Matt. 27 : 25). The deed was done in order that, in the strong language of Cicero, — "*ab oculis, auribusque et omni cogitatione hominum removendum esse,*" — the man might be removed from the sight, hearing, and thought of every one. It is not certain that Satan has any other allies who can serve him as well on the earth as do they who trample upon the body of the Son of God, and count the blood of his covenant an unholy thing, and do despite unto the Spirit of grace (Heb. 10 : 29).

All institutions and corporations which, instead of basing themselves upon the general good, organize the selfishness of men, and give efficiency to that, are powerful instrumentalities in alliance with Satan. Corrupt governments, which oppress the poor, which turn away judgment backward, allow justice to stand afar off, and truth to fall in the street, so that equity can not enter (Is. 59 : 14), are fearful allies of Satan. They are the destructive beasts which appear in apocalyptic vision, with numerous horns, and iron teeth, and breath of fire and smoke, to wound and slay in the earth, and fill it with blasphemies. Still worse, if possible, is a great ecclesiastical institution, by which the supreme selfishness of men is organized into the forms of false religion. With such, the corrupt kings of the earth commit fornication, and the inhabitants of the world are made drunk with the wine furnished at the guilty banquet (Rev. 17: 2). The destructive power of human depravity becomes immensely increased, when, by such establishments, it is combined and centralized.

All systems of infidelity and of unsound philosophy which prevent the "manifestation of the truth" as it is in Christ Jesus, are to be regarded as powerful forces in alliance with Satan.

All that, in man's nature, habits, and circumstances, which Satan can use for the furtherance of his malicious purposes, must be viewed in the same way. If one has a corrupt imagination, a dishonest judgment, a proud heart, a self-will; if one has a tongue which is "set on fire of hell," which "walketh through the earth," and "deviseth mischief like a razor;" if one has a vicious propensity for the bottle, the weed, the dice, or the cards, — he is an ally of Satan, both against himself and all others who can be reached by his example.

But let it not be supposed that the believer's salvation is put in jeopardy, even by the combined power of Satan and his allies. Out of Christ, the case is, indeed, hopeless. In him, it is far otherwise. The Captain of our salvation, omnipotent himself, has abundant allies in the work of our redemption. Every holy mind in the universe is with him; every truth, every conscience, every attribute of man's higher nature, is on his side. The experience of all ages works with him; an innumerable "cloud of witnesses" confirms his gospel; "all power is given unto him;" all knowledge and wisdom are his; all agencies, willingly or by his overruling, shall minister to the truth, and he can not fail to carry into complete and glorious execution the purposes of his love and mercy.

But every man must decide for himself the solemn question whether he will be an eternal ally of Satan, to be cast with him into "the lake of fire," whatever it may be, or become a friend and follower of Christ, and a joint heir with him to the everlasting throne of peace and righteousness, and to all the glories of his kingdom forever. The issue is momentous! Let every man stand in awe before it, and calmly form that decision by which he would have his eternal destiny settled.

CHAPTER XXV.

SATAN THE FOE OF OUR SANCTIFICATION AND GROWTH IN GRACE.

Even as Christ loved the church, and gave himself for it, that he might cleanse it with the washing of water by the word; that he might present it to himself a glorious church, not having spot or wrinkle, or any such thing; but that it should be holy and without blemish. — *Eph.* 5 : 25-27.

DURING the last twenty-five years, unwonted attention has been given to the subject of Christian sanctification, or the "Higher Christian Life." Many, quickened by the discussion, have "left the things which are behind," and advanced from Moses, as their teacher, to Christ and the Spirit, — from the "bondage of the law" to the "liberty of the gospel." It is a hopeful sign of the times that there is an increasing demand for light on this subject. Much that is inspiring has been written; but, instead of exhausting the subject, and satisfying the public mind, it has only opened a mine which invites further exploration.

The writer has supposed that this doctrine might be presented from such a stand-point as would make its truth obvious to Christians of all denominations, clear it from prejudice, and commend it to the joyful acceptance of all the friends of Christ.

18 *

The necessity of a higher standard of holiness admits of but one opinion. Whatever then, may help to make clear the way to a higher religious attainment, to show "what is the greatness of his power to us-ward who believe," and so to counteract the efforts of Satan to hold the church in bondage to the world, ought certainly to be set forth and earnestly pondered.

In order to expose Satan as the foe of our more complete spiritual development, we must first consider what is the divine method of sanctifying the church. This we propose to undertake in several successive sections.

Section I.

Theories of the Different Schools considered, and shown to differ only in Speculative, not Essential Points.

All agree that God requires men to be holy. "Be ye holy, for I am holy," is the changeless command. But there are, growing out of divergent systems of philosophy, three principal methods of interpreting the law of God as the standard of holiness, which give rise to different theories of sanctification.

One class of theologians hold, that man, by the fall, has lost a portion of his ability to love and obey God, and is, therefore, positively unable to obey perfectly the divine law. If a man were to devote to God all the power he has, he would yet fall short of obedience to the law, and remain unholy. But since "without holiness no man shall see the Lord," how is any one to enter heaven? It is replied, by the *imputation* of Christ's righteousness to the believer.

Another class of theologians, with the same underlying philosophy of inability to meet the full claims of the moral law, adopt the idea, as the writer understands, that God has set aside the original precept of his law as the standard of holiness, and given instead thereof, in the gospel, another law leveled to man's present capacities. Obedience to this rule being possible, it is required as the condition of entering heaven, and is holiness.

Another class hold that the law of God adapts itself to all moral agents, whatever their capacities. If they have, by sin, destroyed a part of their power to love God, the law does not still require what they have no power to render. It is insisted that obligation and ability are equal; that the one precept comes to each moral agent in the universe, archangel, angel, fallen angel, man, child, saint or sinner, feeble minded or strong, and says, "Love God with all *thy* heart, with all *thy* might, and with all *thy* strength." The law is a unit, and unchangeable, in the sense of requiring the devotion to God of the whole loving power of each of its innumerable subjects. It is variable, in the sense of requiring different measures of love and service, according to the different capacities of moral beings. To obey the law in this sense, it is said, is to be holy.

Now, these several schools agree, that sinners are to be justified before God only on the ground of Christ's righteousness, never on the ground of their own holiness. It is not material whether this fact be named the doctrine of imputation, or justification by the righteousness of Christ. They agree also in the essential fact, that the condition of salvation is, that the whole heart, all the loving power a man possesses, shall be unreservedly and trustfully surrendered to God; no part of this price may be kept back. The condition is the same in justification, the beginning of the process of salvation, and in sanctification, the carrying forward and completion of the work. The inability to do more is no excuse for refusing to do this.

Princeton, Andover, Oberlin, Newton, and Middletown make precisely the same issue with the sinner. He has broken God's law, and is dead in sin. He can be justified only by devoting his whole being to God, accepting Christ as his Lord and Master, and trusting him for pardon and life. They would also instruct the Christian seeking for sanctification, in the same words: "Devote your whole being to God; accept Christ as your sanctifier by the Holy Spirit, and wait upon him by faith for the blessing." They agree as to the thing, but differ in their philosophy of it. But this is not material.

Here it should be said, that Christians are not called upon to test their characters by either interpretation of the law, technically considered. We are "not under the law," that we must answer *directly* to its claims, but "under grace," that we should be justified by faith in Christ. The practical question for us is this: *Are we truly in Christ*, through compliance with the terms on which he promises salvation? If we are, all is well; for he is to us the "end of the law," and no condemnation, even from Sinai, shall reach us. Our acceptance with the Mediator is perfect. Here, all schools agree.

On the condition necessary to discipleship, Christ undertakes the work of our salvation; to fashion these hearts of ours into temples for his own occupancy, and to make us meet for the inheritance of the saints. Jesus is now the potter, and the believer the *willing* clay. Our salvation, from its incipiency on to its eternally abounding and expanding results in holiness, shall now be wrought in us by the Holy Spirit, who shall change us from glory to glory into the divine image.

Section II.

All Attainments in the Divine Life, the Result of Knowing God in the Heart.

If this proposition be true, it will help to simplify and render clear the whole subject of sanctification. Let us carefully consider it in the light of the Bible.

The New Covenant, the highest and best God has ever made with man, is essentially a promise of life, through the knowledge of himself. "I will put my laws into their minds, and write them in their hearts; and I will be to them a God, and they shall be to me a people," is simply a promise of God that he will so reveal to his people his laws, his truth, his character, that they shall become the ruling forces of their moral being. He will so *reveal himself*, that they will not have to teach each other, saying, "*Know the Lord*," and that they "*shall know him from the least to the greatest*," independently of the imperfect teachings of men, and by the sure light of his Spirit. All the spiritual treasures of the New Testament come, therefore, from knowing the Lord.

Jesus, in his intercessory prayer (John 17 : 3), says, "And this is life eternal, that they might know thee, the only true God, and Jesus Christ, whom thou hast sent." Eternal life here does not mean eternal existence, for knowledge has no tendency to secure that. The wicked, men and devils, exist, but they have not this blessed life. The passage gives us Christ's definition of eternal life, and makes it identical with, or inseparable from knowing God. Its elements, like those of God's own life, are, doubtless, moral purity and holy blessedness. It includes all gracious affections toward God, love, faith, and obedience, in all their modifications. It could not exist, therefore, except as the result of knowing God.

Spiritual life, we are assured by the apostle, originates not from " a corruptible seed, but an incorruptible, even the word of God, which liveth and abideth forever." In order to its being to us the seed of spiritual life, the word of God must, of course, be *made known* to the soul.

The new man is renewed in *knowledge;* and to "grow in grace" is made synonymous with growing "in the *knowledge* of our Lord Jesus Christ" (2 Pet. 3:18; Col. 3:10).

Spiritual infancy and childhood are synonymous with being "unskillful in the *word of righteousness*," while spiritual age and maturity are ascribed only to such as have their spiritual "senses exercised to *discern knowledge*," to know good and evil (Heb. 5: 12-14).

According to Peter (2 Pet. 1:3-5), God, by his divine power, gives us — works into our experience — "*all things that pertain to life and godliness through the knowledge of him that hath called us to glory and virtue.*" Through this knowledge, all the exceeding great and precious promises become ours, to make us partakers of the divine moral nature, and to deliver us from the corruption that is in the world through lust. The promises become life-giving through the knowledge, by the Spirit, of the Promiser.

The passage in 2 Cor. 4:4-6, is very conclusive under this head. It represents Satan as blinding the minds of men through unbelief, "lest the light of the glorious gospel of Christ, who is the image of God," and in whom the "*light of the knowledge of the glory of God*" shines, should reach, and save men from sin and death.

Isaiah saw this truth when he said (53 : 11), "By his knowledge"—i. e., knowledge of him, "shall my righteous servant justify many." Jeremiah understood it too, when he makes God say (3 : 15), "And I will give you pastors according to my heart, which shall feed you with *knowledge* and *understanding*." Paul reflects this view when, in his own experience, he counts all things but loss for the excellency of the knowledge of Christ Jesus his Lord; and where he declares to the Corinthians (1 Cor. 4 : 15), that he has begotten them through the gospel, which he had made known unto them. The apostle John is full of the doctrine also, that he that hath the knowledge of the Son hath life, and he that hath it not hath not life.

On the other hand, Paul (Eph. 4 : 18) affirms that we are alienated from the life of God *through the ignorance* of him, in which sin has involved us; thus showing that the loss of the true knowledge of God brings the death, as the receiving of it, through the Spirit, restores the life promised in the gospel.

To be without God and without hope in the world is to be strangers from the covenants of promise; i. e., to be spiritually ignorant of them (Eph. 2 : 12).

The whole heathen world was given over to corruption and reprobation, on the simple ground that they were unwilling to retain God *in their knowledge* (Rom. 1 : 28); and this not in an arbitrary way, but because such a result was unavoidable where the knowledge of God was not cherished as a living and saving moral force. When Christ comes in flaming fire, it will be to take "vengeance on *those that know not God*" (2 Thess. 1 : 8), showing that their willing ignorance of him is the sin which involves their ruin.

The whole scheme of salvation beautifully harmonizes with this view. The object of God, in revelation, is to acquaint his creatures with himself, that they may be at peace (Job 22 : 21). He leads them through the wilderness that he may *instruct* them. He reveals himself in his word and works, that men may know him and live. He laments over his people that they do not *know* him, not even as well as "the ox knoweth his owner, or the ass his master's crib," that they do not *consider* (Isa. 1 : 3).

The mission of the Spirit, as we shall soon more fully see, is essentially to reveal to the eye of faith the things of Christ as the means of molding the hearts and lives of men into his image from glory to glory, as they reach one degree of knowledge after another. "It doth not yet appear what we shall be," for here we only know in part; and the measure of our life is limited by the measure of our spiritual knowledge; but when he shall appear, and we see him as he is, the fullness of our knowledge of him will then give us the completed life of love and blessedness, of holiness and happiness in heaven.

Section III.

This Knowledge the Exclusive Gift of the Spirit — its Positive and Assuring Nature.

God alone is competent to reveal himself. Unaided human faculties, surely, can not reach the saving knowledge of the Lord. The Scriptures abundantly show that to impart this knowledge is the special mission of the Holy Spirit.

When Peter responded to our Lord's question (Matt. 16: 13-17), by saying, "Thou art the Christ, the Son of the living God," Jesus replied, "Blessed art thou, Simon Bar-jona; for flesh and blood hath not revealed it unto thee, but my Father, which is in heaven." God had himself, then, given to Peter a knowledge of the Messiah which man could not impart; yea, which he could not gain, in the use of his mere human faculties, by holding intercourse with him in the flesh.

Paul says (1 Cor. 12: 3), that "no man can say that Jesus is the Lord but by the Holy Ghost;" meaning, evidently, that no man can say it of his own experimental knowledge, except he has learned it of the Spirit.

The great point which Paul makes, in the second chapter of his first letter to the Corinthians, is, that the things of God can be known only by the Spirit of God. In his natural state, man can not discern them; they are even foolishness to him until spiritually discerned.

We have, in a former chapter, dwelt upon the obvious fact that it is naturally impossible for one being personally to reveal another, and most of all, for a finite one so to make known the Infinite. We conclude, therefore, both with reason and revelation, that God himself is the great and only ultimate source of that divine, life-giving knowledge, on which, from first to last, our salvation depends.

This knowledge of God, which he, by his Spirit, gives, is, moreover, of a *positive* nature; it is *knowledge*. The difference between *knowing* and *surmising* is very great and radical. A man may *suppose* himself to be the heir of a large fortune, and the *hope* that he is so will afford him more or less satisfaction; but when he *knows* it, as he knows he lives, the legacy at once enters into all his experiences, and gives him the consciousness of wealth. All sense of poverty disappears, and the good which money can bestow becomes a matter of natural and habitual enjoyment.

Now, this *knowledge* of our inheritance in Christ is what the church most of all needs. It is what she can and ought to have. It is by the same laws of mind, that, when God, in all his blessed, life-giving relations to ourselves, is made *known* to us, his precious truths enter into all our experiences, into our very life, shape our characters, and determine all our moral unfoldings. Both the heart and the outward life are influenced by them. Falling short of this real knowledge, we can only speculate about God; we can *guess* that this is true, and that is false; we can believe that he will do this, and will not do that; but such views can give the soul no life, no resurrection from the death of sin, no salvation.

But some will say, "How *can* the Spirit make us to *know* the things of God, so as to lift us up from doubt to assurance?" It may help some minds to consider this question, although it may be difficult to understand the *how*, before the spiritual illumination is actually enjoyed.

We do know some things in a way that excludes all uncertainty. We thus know the axiom, that the whole of a thing is greater than any of its parts, and the principle, that every event must have a cause. We know our own existence, and that we have the power of thought, feeling, and action.

With this faculty of certain, intuitive knowledge, which we call the reason, the mind apprehends some things directly. They stand out so openly and unmistakably that we want no proof of them. We see them with a clearness which no reasoning can increase. God, with his omniscient eye, sees all things in this way, and has no need of intermediate steps to gain knowledge of any kind. But it is not so with us. What we do not see intuitively, we are to learn by other means. We resort to the reasoning process, and by this we may often gain the same certainty of knowledge, as when we apprehend it by the eye of reason. Indeed, the reasoning process is nothing but the effort of the mind to bring objects before this faculty of certain knowledge — a sort of telescope, by the use of which we would bring such objects within the mind's range of vision. The syllogism is a kind of ladder on which we run up for the sake of a better and wider view. The reasoning we adopt may not always bring us the assured knowledge we seek; the ladder may be too short, or the telescope may not have sufficient power, or we may fail to point it correctly; but it can not be denied that we gain some certain knowledge by our reasoning processes. Some truth becomes thus *manifested* to the faculty of certain knowledge, to the exclusion of all disturbing doubt and anxiety. The mind is assured and at rest.

But, beyond all that we can learn by our reasoning powers, we have the explicit and positive promise of God, that *he will make himself known to us*. It is not material that we should know just how the Spirit can make real to us the manifestation of divine things. He is pledged to do it, and this is enough. Surely, He who has given us the power to know, will not fail to give us the promised knowledge. He that hath made the eye, shall he not cause it to see? Yes, he will give the soul a knowledge of himself on which we can rest, as on the bosom of the Infinite. Doubt will die, and the soul shall say with Job, "I *know* that my Redeemer liveth," and shall feel the glorious pulsations of eternal life throbbing through all the channels of its being.

The Spirit may, of course, employ all methods of communicating the things of God to the soul. He may exhibit them directly to the eye of the reason, or through the written word, or by his providences; through his works, as we look on flower or dew-drop below, or the stars above, or, through our processes of reasoning.

When the disciples asked Jesus how he could manifest himself to them, and not be seen by the world, he explained the promise by saying, that he and the Father would come and make their abode with them. In other words, the manifestation should be as real as that of the friends with whom we dwell. They did not understand from the promise of the manifestation how much it meant; but when it came on the day of Pentecost, they *knew* it all.

Human minds may, and they often do, know each other with an assurance which results in a happy unity of trust and love. Let it not be doubted, then, that the divine and human mind may know each other with a more perfect assurance, and with far higher and richer results.

Section IV.

Conditions of Receiving this Life-giving Knowledge of God. — A Theological Difficulty met.

Of faith, as the great Bible condition of salvation, we shall speak hereafter. We wish now to call attention to some things which are included in faith, but which need a distinct notice.

There must, then, be in the mind a substantially correct idea of Christianity, as appears from the sketch in Chapter XI. The right knowledge of God logically produces the true Christian life in the soul, and no other. But if a man's idea is, that piety consists in a mere hope of heaven, in pleasurable religious emotions, in good wishes toward God and man, or in the performance of certain external duties, instead of a real *moral oneness* with God, he will unconsciously modify the knowledge of God as it comes to his mind, to make it harmonize with his idea, and promote what he calls piety. He will deceive himself, and build on the sand. If, on the other hand, he has the true idea, the knowledge of God as he is will meet his case, and secure its own legitimate result, the true Christian life. We must, then, start with the conception, that to serve and honor God, to do his will, to reflect his truth, to accept the suffering and the blessing he may appoint us, *with himself for our portion*, is the one and only business of our existence. Every thing else is subordinate to this, and included in it.

There must be intense hungering and thirsting after the knowledge of God. "If thou criest after knowledge, and liftest up thy voice for understanding, — if thou seekest her as silver, and searchest for her as for hid treasures, — then shalt thou understand the fear of the Lord, *and find the knowledge of God* (Prov. 2 : 3–5). It is well known how eagerly men seek after gold. When, in like way, they put their whole heart upon finding the saving knowledge of God, they have this express promise that they *shall* find it.

There must be also the teachable spirit — a readiness to obey all truth as soon as discovered. The pupil must bow implicitly to the Divine Teacher in the exercise of a child-like and reverent spirit, for this is the key which opens the door to the incoming of knowledge. The will must be submissive and true.

Some theologians may start a difficulty here thus: To have the will brought into this state of submission is only possible as the result of knowing God, and yet you make it the condition of knowing him. Do you not, then, require salvation as the condition of salvation? If you say the will must *first* be submissive in order to saving knowledge, and if only this very knowledge can bring the will into this state, then how is salvation possible?

Reply: The submission of the will to the light it

has is not the whole of salvation, any more than the determination of a hungry man to eat offered food is the whole of salvation to the body from starvation. The food must be eaten and assimilated. Again: that special knowledge of God which gives eternal life is not the only knowledge of God which the soul needs, and to which the will must bow. Every mind has some light by nature; and we know the condition of having more is, that we submit to and follow that. The promise is, that we shall know savingly "if we follow on to know." The Spirit has a double ministry. One part of his mission is to give a knowledge of God which works condemnation, convicts of sin, sweeps away excuses, destroys self-righteous hope, induces repentance and turning to God. This done, another and higher part of his mission is to take of the things of Jesus and show them unto us — to manifest God in Christ to the inner man, his truth, his love, in a way to put us in possession of the very life of God from which sin has alienated us, thus completing the process of our spiritual birth. The first part of the Spirit's work is the condition of the second. According to the distinction of President Edwards, the former is the Spirit's work *on* the mind, the latter *in* it. To know some things about God, works repentance, submission, hope; to know other things, gives life, peace, and joy in the Holy Ghost.

Not only does the mode of the Spirit with the sinner change, at the point of submission and repentance, but the radical position of the sinner himself is changed. He occupies an entirely new stand-point. To that which he now sees, he was blind before. Truth has displaced falsehood from his mind; all God's truths, all the precious exhibitions of his love and goodness in his works and word, have now their proper adjustment before his mind; and, as the Spirit lays open to his inner view their deep and eternal significance, and gives him something of God's own conception of benevolence and mercy, the currents of eternal life flow sweetly, or roll deeply, or surge resistlessly through all the domain of his moral and spiritual being.

Too much importance can not be attached to maintaining an inflexibly obedient will, as the condition of all spiritual life and knowledge.

Section V.

The Relations of Revealed Truth to our Growing Sanctification.

The prayer of Christ for his people is, "Sanctify them through thy truth; thy word is truth." The word here referred to is, doubtless, the written revelation.

In considering this topic, we must discriminate between the truth as a mere form of words, and as a moral power working the sanctification of the soul. Words, in themselves, are mere signs which are used to give expression to thought, and feeling, and purpose. When men use words, a human meaning only is put into them, and they express only what is finite, weak, and imperfect. When God uses them, they express and convey his infinite thought and purpose. "Let there be light" gave expression to the divine omnipotence, and created the worlds. His word, when he issues it, opens the sea or closes it; it executes his will. It carries with it the whole mind-force of Jehovah.

The Bible is written in the language of men; and the subtle influence of unbelief leads them, too often, to attach only a human significance to it. They read it as if it expressed only what one finite mind can express to another; and thus the gospel ceases to be the power of God unto salvation — the promises of Christ weigh and mean no more than the promises of men. The Bible reveals the truth as far as mere words can do it. But something is demanded beyond the words themselves. Let God use these words of Holy Scripture, let the Divine Spirit set them vibrating on our mental ear as with the voice of the Almighty, so that they shall express and manifest to the soul *God's own state of mind*, his love, his infinite power and excellence, his nearness, his relations to us and ours to him, and then they carry with them an infinitude of spiritual and saving energy, of which the soul partakes unto its sanctification. The gospel is no longer the word of man, but the power and wisdom of God himself to all who receive it.

The Scriptures, then, consist of a collection of words as symbols, through which God seeks to reveal himself, and lay open his mind and heart to men, for their sanctification. But these words or symbols become effective to this end only when the Holy Spirit is heard speaking through them to the heart of faith.

SECTION VI.

The Relation between knowing God by the Spirit, and the Enjoyment of the Life of Holiness.

In the first place, it will not be doubted that God has constituted us for the enjoyment of spiritual blessedness, of life in all its fullness and perfection.

We know that he has made the human, in the image and likeness of the divine mind. Our mental and moral faculties are so like God's, that we may be in our measure, as he calls us to be, like him. We can reason with him, prove him, think his thoughts, and conform to his will. The same things, therefore, which constitute the moral life, the holy blessedness and purity of God, will, when attained, constitute ours. To have the "life of God" is but to have his state of mind. To live for the same end, to love supremely what he so loves, to hate what he hates, to prefer and receive his thoughts, feelings, and purposes as our own, will as certainly give us eternal life, as they give it to him.

And, again, the object he has in manifesting himself to us is, evidently, to beget in us, in our measure, his own character and experiences. He aims to make us partakers of his will, his motives, his ends, and, so, of the "divine nature." The especial work of the Spirit is, by giving us the knowledge of God, to change us into his moral image and life, from glory to glory, and thus to fit us to enjoy him forever.

From all this it follows conclusively, that, so far forth as we receive the true knowledge of God obediently from the Holy Spirit, the enjoyment of the promised eternal life is a fixed and glorious result; we must become joyful partakers of his holiness, his patience, his love, his blessedness.

Section VII.

The Natural and Life-giving Effect upon the Mind of knowing, from Heaven, certain Definite Things concerning God and ourselves — concerning His Relations to us and ours to Him.

We have just seen that the knowledge of God, by the Spirit, carries with it the elements of eternal life to the soul. Let us, then, consider the natural result of so knowing certain specific things.

Take, first, the knowledge that our sins are all forgiven, and blotted from the book of God's remembrance. If the way of the Spirit with a man has been to penetrate him deeply with a knowledge of his guilt; if he has seen its exceeding sinfulness; if the law has come home to him as it came to Paul, annihilating his self-righteousness, and impaling his trembling soul upon the points of its burning wrath; if he has been made to see himself in the men who cried, "Crucify him, crucify him," or in him who struck the death-spear to the Savior's heart; if he has seen the great river of righteous blood, which, from the days of Abel, sin has shed, flooding his soul with all its guilt because he had rejected and despised Him who alone could stay that flood; and then learns, from the Holy Spirit, that his sin is all forgiven him, and washed away in that Redeemer's blood, — he will naturally have an experience of the greatest intensity. To know that *he* — such a wretch — is redeemed and adopted into the family of God, and sealed for eternal glory, must go far to reconstruct his character, and develop in his soul a new and divine life.

Take, again, the simple fact of God's loving and abiding presence, sweetly manifested as a reality to the soul's inner consciousness. The result is, that we know and feel, that we live, and move, and have our being in him, as the body lives, and moves, and has its being in the atmosphere which surrounds it. The soul communes with him as with an intimate, present friend. Prayer is no longer an effort to address God in the distant heavens, but is as natural, and easy, and spontaneous as the communion, face to face, of loving friends. It is not limited to particular hours and forms, but goes on very much as two kindred and loving minds, dwelling together, will, by the laws of want and suggestion, and by the very tendency of love to communicate, be always expressing themselves to each other.

This presence of God may sometimes dazzle and almost blind the soul with its effulgence, as with Moses when God showed him something of his glory. But, generally, the Lord will so manifest his presence that it will be to the soul, what the air is to the body, the natural, healthy, life-giving, and most satisfying element in which it is possible to live. When, by this manifestation, the believer's heart becomes the Shekinah wherein Jehovah dwells, it must have a life rich with all heavenly elements.

In this knowledge of God's glorious presence, there is a power to save of immeasurable magnitude. Nothing can so nearly extinguish temptation as this. It fortifies the soul at all points; it overcomes that unsatisfied state of the mind which is the hope and strength of the adversary; it removes the darkness of sin, and strips the disguises from the father of lies. "Moses endured as seeing Him who is invisible." It is in the felt absence of the Deliverer that we are exposed to the rake of temptation. When

Jesus was taken by his murderers from the disciples, so that they were "in that hour" deprived of his conscious and sympathizing presence, they all forsook him and fled before the storm. They knew not yet his invisible, spiritual nearness; but, on the day of Pentecost, when he was thus manifested to them, one could chase a thousand, and two put ten thousand to flight. Nothing could stand before them when they knew God's presence as a wall of fire round about and a glory overshadowing them.

When, in addition to this, God comes to be known in his omniscience, omnipotence, and eternity; when he discloses himself in his moral attributes, his infinite benevolence and love, his wisdom, his justice, his mercy, and his patience, there results to the believer a fullness of life which makes him exclaim, "O the depth of the riches, both of the wisdom and knowledge of God! How unsearchable are his judgments, and his ways past finding out!"

Take, again, that fact revealed in the gospel, that God unites himself to us in all blessed relations, as the branch is united to the vine; that he makes his own life the source and wasteless fountain of ours, and ordains that, because he lives, we shall live also. To know this oneness with him, by the Holy Spirit, is full of immortality. It is no longer a cold, constructive union, formed by some spiritual mechanics, or by some abstract governmental arrangement, which carries no living power with it, but a vital reality in the soul's conscious life. We know our espousals to God; faith celebrates the marriage, and we are in heaven, as it were, before the time. The consciousness is blessed! It is not a rag-picker married to a millionnaire, and dwelling in his palace, enjoying his smile and confidence, bearing his name, sharing his wealth and his position, delighting in his love, and resting under his protection; but, more than that, a sinner who was all stained with guilt and shame, now redeemed and washed in atoning blood, and wedded to the King of heaven, dwelling in his glorious banqueting house, enjoying his smile, bearing his honored name and his seal, shielded by his arm, and chosen as the object of his tenderest affection.

By virtue of this union, we are one with Christ as he and the Father are one; and the same glory which the Father gave him, he gives to us. Jesus becomes our ever-living Intercessor, our Prophet, and High-Priest, our Surety, our Passover, our Advocate; and is "made of God unto us wisdom, righteousness, sanctification, and redemption." And when all this comes to be manifested to us by the Spirit, and we learn, by his teaching, that "all the fullness of the Godhead" dwells in Christ, that we may be "complete in him," of course there results to the soul a life and a blessedness which "passeth knowledge."

Take, still again, the Father's wonderful love to the Son, on account of which he can and will bestow the richest of his blessings, without measure, upon Christ's trustful and loving followers. To know this by the Spirit is important in order to overcome the tendency to make our own worthiness our plea at the mercy-seat, and that we may apprehend the infinite weight there is in that argument, "*for Christ's sake,*" which we urge in all our prayers. Let us, on this point, draw an illustration from a passage of

Sacred History.

The friendship of David and Jonathan was disinterested and beautiful. Jonathan gave up his own claims to the throne, incurred the wrath of his father, and periled his own life, to secure to David, whom the Lord had appointed, the scepter of the kingdom. David did not forget this kindness of his friend. Soon after he was crowned, he gathered his court around him, and inquired thus: "Is there any that is left of the house of Saul, that I may show him kindness for Jonathan's sake?" The answer was equivocal. He was merely told that there was still living an old servant of Saul, by the name of Ziba. The king at once ordered Ziba to be brought before him. Fixing his eager eye upon him, David pressed the question upon the servant: "Is there not yet any of the house of Saul, that I may show the kindness of God unto him?" Ziba, hesitatingly, stammered out the fact, that Jonathan himself had a son yet living, but he was lame in both his feet, unable to stand, and unworthy of the king's notice. David learned where he was, and immediately dispatched an officer to bring him. When he came into the royal presence, he fell on his face and did reverence. The king addressed him by his name, Mephibosheth, and said, "Fear not; for I will surely show thee kindness, for Jonathan thy father's sake." Mephibosheth bowed himself, and, as expressive of his sense of unworthiness, said, "What is thy servant, that thou shouldst look upon such a dead dog as I am?" But David heeded not his words; he had found his man, and was only thinking what expression he could give of his love to Jonathan by blessing his poor, worthless, crippled son. And what does he do? In the first place, he bestows upon him all the property and possessions which had belonged to the house of Saul; and, not to encumber the poor man with the care of them, he appoints Ziba, and his family, and servants to manage the estates for Mephibosheth. And in the second place, he ordains that Mephibosheth himself shall dwell in Jerusalem, in the royal family, and sit with the king at his table, as one of the king's sons, as long as he lives (2 Sam. 9).

Thus did David illustrate his love to Jonathan; and the illustration is all the more forcible and significant by reason of the miserable condition of Mephibosheth.

My argument here is this: If David, on account of

his mere human and imperfect love to Jonathan, would bestow so great gifts upon poor, crippled Mephibosheth, as a testimony of that love, what may we not expect our Heavenly Father will do for us, the lame and worthless Mephibosheths, disciples of Jesus, on account of his infinite and perfect devotion to his well-beloved and only begotten Son? There is no limit to what he will do. He will give us, not merely what pertained to Saul and his house, but all things. Mark his words: "All things are yours; whether Paul, or Apollos, or Cephas, or the world, or life, or death, or things present, or things to come; all are yours." "How shall he not with him freely give us all things?" And more than this, he adopts us into his family, as the King's sons, joint-heirs with the First Born himself, that we may eat our meat at the royal table, at the King's right hand forever. Nor does he heed the fact, that we are more unworthy and worse wounded than was the son of Jonathan.

Then, there was no special reason, outside of his mere love to Jonathan, why David should thus attest his affection for him. But there are grave reasons, aside from the impulse there is in love to manifest itself, why the Father should let the universe see his infinite appreciation of his Son. His enemies have denied his Deity, and maligned his character. They have treated him as an impostor, as a deceiver, even as a "prince of devils," and as wholly unworthy of the confidence and affection of his creatures. They have sought to alienate from his love and service, his children, redeemed by his blood, and to rob him of all his glory. When he was in the flesh, they hated him and cursed him; and, that they might cover his name with eternal infamy, and root his memory out of the earth, they put him to the shameful death of the cross. And shall not the Almighty Father let those enemies and the whole universe see how he regards his Son? Can he fail to do any thing, in kind or degree, by which he can attest his love to Jesus, and exalt his name above all other names in earth or in heaven? And surely there is no way in which he can so fitly and forcibly show his love to his Son, as by enriching with wealth incorruptible the poor, crippled disciples of that Son who are still struggling against his enemies and theirs on the earth. When it shall be seen that the Father, *for Christ's sake*, concentrates all blessing, for time and eternity, upon such poor Mephibosheths, setting them upon his throne, and making his own glory appear in them in its fullness, then hell will be confounded, and every knee — willingly or unwillingly — will bow, and every tongue confess that "Jesus Christ is Lord, to the glory of God the Father."

The strength of God's moral government lies essentially in the character of Christ; for that character is God's own, manifested as a power to mold his creatures into his own moral likeness. All the issues of that government over a universe of minds, therefore, stand out as reasons to the heart of God for exalting his only begotten Son. How certain it is, then, that, for reasons altogether independent of our worthiness, God will bestow upon us, as the disciples of Christ, all things in earth and heaven, the giving of which can testify his love toward his Son.

It seems to the writer, that the knowledge of these things, by the Spirit, must be equivalent to a *carte blanche* — a letter of credit — allowing us to draw upon God, *for Christ's sake*, for whatever the true interests of the soul, in its inner and higher life, can, in any contingency, require. It brings to us the "fullness of the blessing of the gospel of Christ."

Consider, again, the Spirit's assurance of this one principle and law of God's administration, that "*all things shall work together for good to them that love God.*" To *know* this establishes one's feet upon solid rock; it gives a constant and universal victory to faith. Does your companion fall at your side? is the babe plucked from your arms? has misfortune swept away all your estate? You *know* all shall work for *good*, and can easily smile through your tears, and gratefully kiss the rod. Does Satan assault you with temptation to tear you away from Jesus? You can coolly look him in the eye, and say, "Satan, I know you, and that you would destroy my soul. I have no strength of my own to contend successfully with you; but the Holy Ghost has shown me, and I *know* that Jesus is my Deliverer, and that he will make all things work together for my good. The battle is not mine, but his (2 Chron. 20 : 15). If God will use your temptations as polishing stones wherewith to burnish my character, develop my faith, and give me a fuller knowledge of himself, the gain will be mine, not yours." Thus the disciple can sing the pean of victory even before the battle is fought.

The Bible is full of principles and truths, the knowledge of which, by the Spirit, will, in like way, fortify the soul, and open fountains in the deserts and rivers in the dry places. In this way, all "the exceeding great and precious promises" become words of life and power. Like the distributing pipes for water and gas, in a great city, they carry the water and light of life into all the departments of our being. The promises are God's seals; and when the Holy Spirit writes (Heb. 8 : 10) on the heart of the believer, "Into all places whithersoever thou goest, I will be with thee," he may travel round the world, and carry with him every where the consciousness of his Savior's presence. Let the Spirit say to the believer, — as once he said to a young man, who, with his heart full of light and love, and wondering whether Jesus would abide with him, opened his "Daily Food," and found this promise recorded for the day, —" Unto your old age I am he; and even to hoar hairs will I carry you : I have made and I will bear; even I will carry and will deliver you"

(Is. 46 : 4) ; or this, "I will never, no, never leave thee, nor forsake thee," and he will have no occasion to go to Calvin to learn the doctrine of the saints' perseverance ; he knows it from above. He is sealed, and no man shall pluck him from his Father's hand.

The blessedness, which the spiritual knowledge of these and other things innumerable gives to the soul, is rich beyond the power of human language or imagery to describe. The Celestial City of Bunyan, the New Jerusalem of John, with all its gorgeous and golden streets, its pearly gates and precious stones, its crystal waters and trees of life, is but a shadowy representation, after all, of the reality. It is as good as material things can give ; but still the fact remains, that "eye hath not seen, nor ear heard, nor have entered into the heart of man, the things which God hath prepared for them that love him."

President Edwards has a beautiful description of the soul enjoying these divine illuminations. It is "like a field or garden of God, with all manner of pleasant flowers, enjoying a sweet calm, and the gentle, vivifying beams of the sun — like such a little flower as we see in the spring of the year, low and humble on the ground, opening its bosom to receive the pleasant beams of the sun's glory ; rejoicing, as it were, in a calm rapture ; diffusing around a sweet fragrancy ; standing peacefully and lovingly in the midst of other flowers round about, all, in like manner, opening their bosoms to drink in the light of the sun."

Section VIII.

The Law of Progress in this Divine, Saving Knowledge; with a Sketch illustrating the Spirit's Method. — The "Higher Christian Life" explained.

Nothing is more certain than that we gain spiritual knowledge, as we do all other, by degrees. Many lessons occupy the mind a long time, before we fully know them. The Spirit hints at things and puts the mind on inquiry; and the hungry heart searches for the truth as for hid treasures, and is blessed in searching. Sometimes the Spirit will make knowledge break in suddenly upon the mind, as the traveler, arrived at some mountain top, is in an instant ravished with a new and wonderful panorama; at others, he causes it to dawn after the manner of the sun's rising, dimly at first, but with increasing power and glory till it reaches the meridian.

Our advancement in the divine life will be, on the whole, as our advancement in the spiritual apprehension of God and divine things. This may be taken as the law of spiritual progress.

It makes a man a Christian to know Christ as forgiving him his sins, and giving him hope of heaven through his blood. In his conversion, a sinner sees his lost condition, and casts himself trustingly and unreservedly upon Christ as his Savior. He runs well for a season, glad that he is hopefully in the kingdom of God, that Christ will be his Advocate at the judgment, and receive him at last to dwell at his own right hand.

But the young convert soon finds that he has need of something more. The world overcomes him. His passions are not effectually crucified. Pride lifts its head. Mammon finds place in his heart. Foes assail him from without and from within, and he seems to himself to be in the mouth of the lion, or in the paws of the bear. Darkness comes over him, difficulties lie in his path, and, in his fear, he is perchance almost ready to blame his Moses for leading him forth from his house of bondage. Like the Israelites of old, he is " discouraged by reason of the way." Many yield to temptation here, and never come to the table of the Lord. They do not, however, forget their hope of pardon, but, in their trouble, flee to it as their city of refuge. Others, more resolute, make profession of religion, but they make little progress, and are unsatisfied.

Now, the difficulty is, that these beginners in the school of Christ have only taken their first lesson. *It is a new lesson they require.* They do not yet know that Christ is with them *now*, ever present to deliver them from their enemies without and their fears within, and to give them grace to serve him " in holiness and righteousness all the days of their life " (Luke 2 : 68–80). They are in the condition of the disciples between the betrayal of Christ and the baptism of the Holy Ghost, when they all forsook him and fled. They are often sad and disappointed as they journey to Emmaus, wondering at all the things which have happened in their experience, and not knowing that the Master, by his Spirit, is talking with them by the way. Some, perhaps, recalling certain words of Christ, and hastening to the sepulcher, find he is risen, and tell the story of their new joy to others. But their words seem to these as idle tales. They are bewildered, and know not what to do. Thomas will not believe till he can put his finger into the prints of the nails, and his hand into the Savior's side. But the Lord is risen indeed, and begins at length to "open their understandings, that they may understand the Scriptures." Light dawns; the dispensation of the Spirit is at hand; the disciples are now tarrying in Jerusalem in an upper room, waiting for the promise of the Father.

This brings us to the second stage of spiritual knowledge. Thanks be to God, *the Spirit comes* and imparts to them *the knowledge of Jesus as a present and Almighty Savior*. The scales drop from their eyes; they see Jesus present with them; they know that he is God, and that all saving power on earth and in heaven is given him in their behalf. They see him now with the eye of faith as the eye of sense could not see him when in the body. He will no more appear and disappear, as he did in his flesh, but abide with them forever. The crucifixion and the grave have not taken him from them, as they had supposed, but have only brought him nearer, and disclosed him to them in all his divine fullness and power. They speak with tongues of fire, for they but utter the thoughts of the indwelling Spirit. Now, too, they are strong, and enriched with abounding grace. Peter, who quailed before a Jewish maiden, now fears not the Sanhedrim, and would indeed die sooner than deny his Master.

What is termed the *"Higher Christian Life"* is reached. The Lord Jesus, the Mighty God, the Savior, is made known by the Spirit as ever present with the disciples as their life and their strength, their salvation and their Deliverer; and why should they longer fear what man can do unto them?

But this is only another stage in divine knowledge. The soul is yet exposed to temptation, as was Jesus himself, and must learn how to appropriate the new salvation so as to gain the victory; or, in other words, the soul must come to know God in his methods of saving us from the power of our enemies. For example, suppose a man to be assaulted with impure and lustful thoughts, which, if indulged, would lead to sin. They would be exceedingly disgusting and hateful to his renewed sensibility. He would resist them, but could not exorcise them; they would not go at *his* bidding. He knows that Jesus is with him to save. Let the tempted disciple go to him for a specific victory. He will give it. But how? He will bestow *his own knowledge of the subject* on his disciple; he will give him *his idea* in making the race male and female, and it shall take out of his mind all that which ever made him "look on a woman to lust after her," and give him that purity of heart in which "all things are" seen to be "pure." The deliverance will be glorious; and this specific cleansing of his sensibility by divine knowledge will intensify his love of his Redeemer, and enlarge his capacity for usefulness in his service.

In like way, suppose the mind to be tempted to pride. The remedy is not in any strength of our own, gained by a general sense of the Savior's presence with us, to overcome it. We need to know our infinite Redeemer specifically with reference to the temptation to be proud. Let him give us *his idea* of pride and humility; let him reveal himself to us in the act of washing the disciples' feet, in the process of making himself of no reputation, of humbling himself from King of kings and Lord of lords to servant of servants; let him give us the knowledge of God as serving his enemies, at the sacrifice of his own life on the cross—and the work is done. We shall see pride as never before, and our hearts will gravitate toward lowliness—"all lowliness."

If the Lord would show us our weakness, and make us feel our ignorance, and that we are less than the least of all things, he has but to manifest himself to the willing and waiting heart in his omnipotence and in his omniscience: the contrast must bring us speedily to the dust. If he would reconcile us to the deepest poverty, he can accomplish it by showing us himself, emptied of all riches that he might make them abound to others. If he would strengthen us to love our enemies and bless those that curse us, he need only unfold the glory there is, to his view, in doing it.

Is any real disciple troubled lest his unworthiness should, after all, exclude him from heaven, — let the Holy Spirit reveal to him the righteousness of Christ wherein he stands, and he shall know that his acceptance by the Father, for Christ's sake, will be as perfect as if he were the chief of the apostles.

In what words can be described the soul's holy rapture, when God makes himself known to it in his infinite love? or its profound awe and self-abasement, when Jehovah unvails himself in his infinite holiness and justice? or its quiet and grateful submission, when he appears in all his infinite patience? or its abhorrence of sin and unbelief, when God discloses his idea of their heinousness? or its love for souls, when God testifies to it of their value, and reveals the boundlessness of his own compassion for them?

There is no end, of course, to the unfoldings which God may make to his redeemed of the glorious riches of his character; of the infinitude of his natural attributes; of the wealth and royal condescension of his love; of the holy tenderness of his patience; of the awful firmness of his justice; of the richness and freeness of his mercy; of all the wasteless treasures of his grace; of the incomprehensible minuteness, as well as vastness, of his works; and of the sublimity and grandeur of all his purposes and of his government. But these unfoldings will go on as the rolling ages pass away, and we shall be transfigured by them, and be wrought into a more and more enlarged and perfect unity with the Lord our God forever. We add

A Sketch, illustrating the Spirit's Method of bringing the Soul to the Knowledge of God.

A young man was hopefully converted to Christ while engaged in business in Western New York. Pressed in his conscience with the duty of preaching the gospel, he excused himself in one way and another, till he was married and settled in life. *Then* it seemed safe, in urging other young men to go, to say, "I would go without hesitation but for my family and my business." He committed himself over and over again in this way, in circumstances where the Holy Ghost was, to him, a conscious witness of his word. The Lord had thus taken him unawares, for it was but a short work for God to call the young wife to himself, and open a door out of the house of merchandise. There was no longer any escape from the call of duty but to rebel against God, and become a liar to the Holy Ghost. He went. While reading Virgil, and Horace, and Xenophon, he read also James Brainard Taylor. It was clear that that man had received an anointing from God which he needed, above all learning, to qualify him to preach the gospel. Could he have it? He believed he could, and set his heart upon it. He began to inquire at the mercy-seat for the way. The Spirit seemed to answer thus: "First, run your eye back over your past life, and find what has been wrong, and set it right — confess — restore." This work was undertaken. Things then assumed a peculiar look. An umbrella taken carelessly, in place of one's own, was stolen. Breaking a just law was wronging every citizen of the nation; and no matter that it was fashionable, and that others did it, and even the officers of the law winked at it. Injustice in the least was injustice in much. "Trifling sins" were no longer trifles. When this work was done, one step toward the blessing seemed taken. "What next, Lord?" was now the inquiry. Here the answer came, "Whosoever he be of you that forsaketh not all that he hath can not be my disciple." And must all — friends, property, life — be laid upon the altar and given up to God in such a sense as to transfer the ownership, and leave the disciple, henceforth, a simple and conscious *steward* of God, to use his life, and whatever he should possess, for his glory? This was reasonable, and ought to be done. The student paused to weigh the matter. Could he do it? It was a serious question. To blot out the *I*, and give its place to *Christ*, in the whole life, was a very comprehensive act. No more to live, but to let Christ live in him, was the great requirement. To say it, was not enough. The *I*, the dear *ego*, must be nailed to the cross. The student struggled with himself in this counting of the cost of building his tower. He had given up his business and a good prospect of wealth, to become a minister. And must he now go deeper, and give up his very life and identity, as it were, to Christ, in order to obtain the anointing, without which his ministry would be barren and irksome? At length he felt himself ready for the great sacrifice. He bowed at the mercy-seat, and, deliberately and formally, made the consecration. It was a pleasant hour. For a little, it seemed as if the work had been effectually done. But ere long, some test from the Spirit revealed the fact that the *I* still occupied the place which had been in words, even honestly used, offered to Christ. The whole ground was gone over again, more solemnly and carefully, — yes, again and again, — with the same failure for a result. The act of consecration *did not hold*. The young man was distressed and perplexed with his failure, and knew not what to do. He carried the case to the great Teacher. The Spirit came to his relief, and showed him that *he* was attempting, by this effort at consecration in his own strength, to cast down the *I*, that *Christ* might come and take the throne in its stead. The reigning sovereign did not succeed in deposing himself. The eye of faith as yet but recognized Christ *in the distance*, ready, indeed, to come *in* when the *I* was driven *out;* but this dethronement, without the power of Christ, was impossible. This gulf between the soul and the Savior *in the distance*, must be bridged, or there could be no relief. Now, the Spirit opened up the fact that the Deliverer was *not* waiting in the distance, but was *near*, even now in the believer's heart, and that nothing remained but by faith to drop into his outstretched arms, and leave him *to take* the offered throne, and, by his power, dethrone the usurper. The difficulty was removed. The disciple responded, "Yea, thou present Almighty One, *take the throne*, and do thy pleasure." The thing was done. The consecration held, as it did not before, and there was a sweet assurance of acceptance. Another great step was evidently taken: the soul was in a blessed place, but yet something more was wanting. There were quietness and peace, but there was unsatisfied hunger. The Spirit's instruction now was, "Wait on the Lord;" "Look to Jesus." The young man waited, O, how eagerly! — even as the eleven in that upper room at Jerusalem. Ere long, *the Holy Spirit took away the vail*, and he found himself in the living presence of God, his Savior. He saw and was in the glory of God. He seemed in a new world, with new heavens and a new earth. The Lamb was the light thereof. The immediate presence of Jesus was not less real than if he had been visible to the outward eye. He had come and *manifested* himself according to his promise; and, in the heart of that disciple, there were exceeding great joy and fullness of glory. He had not seen, nor heard, nor conceived before, what God had provided for them that love him. His soul was full, satisfied, and could ask no more. That for which he had hungered long was more than realized. This same glory which was in the believer's heart shone upon the pages of revelation, and showed every promise instinct with the very life and power of God to his soul. The Book became a living book; its words, living and life-giving words. It shone equally on the world without, so that it was seen to be indeed "full of the glory of God." Christ was all and in all, and all was well.

To the subsequent experience of this individual, we shall refer again in our closing chapter, in which the great fight with and victory over Satan will be drawn out.

Section IX.

What may we reasonably hope to attain in this Life, in Respect to the State, (1.) Of the Will; (2.) Of the Intellect; (3.) Of the Sensibility; — or in the Matter of Purpose, Knowledge, and Emotion?

In view of the method of salvation here defined,

what may we reasonably hope to attain while we remain in the flesh?

Perhaps no fixed rule of attainments can be given. God may, for special and sovereign reasons, so reveal himself to a Paul, a Luther, or an Edwards, as to secure attainments in them entirely beyond the experience of the mass of Christians. Then, the progress of individuals may depend very much upon themselves. The earnest pupils of the Spirit will, naturally and surely, distance the more indifferent ones.

Certainly, no one may hope to reach a state where he can stand by his own powers, where he may cease to depend entirely and alone on Christ, or where there will be no further growth in grace. Certainly, no one may hope, in this life, to attain a state where there will be no more exposure to temptation. Christ was exposed to it to the last, and died in the midst of it.

But we may hope, *as to the Will*, that, through this divine knowledge of Christ, it will become so devoted to him that it will cease, knowingly, to swerve from its fidelity. It may so far overcome temptation as to remain inflexible up to the point of saying, in its Gethsemane of trial, "Nevertheless, not my will, but thine be done," or of dying a shameful death, crying, "*Eloi, eloi, lama sabachthani.*" The will often becomes inflexible in its devotion to earthly friends; why not to the infinite, heavenly

Friend? Why should not the martyr spirit be common to Christians? With the presence of the Deliverer realized; with the promise of victory over temptation sealed to the soul; with the terrible criminality of transgression seen in the light of God's revealed holiness; with the lesson learned from the Spirit that *to believe is to conquer;* with the consciousness that fidelity of will to God is not only "the greatest apparent good," but that, without such fidelity, there is no other possible good; with the lies and disguises of Satan exposed, — why should not the will stand inflexibly true to God, ever turning to him as the needle to the pole? Why not be habitually fixed, "unmovable, always abounding in the work of the Lord"? A brother recently illustrated his views to me on this question by stating how his own mind worked in a given case. He had an only daughter, who was his life, so far as a child can be the life of a parent. She sickened, and trembled between two worlds. The Savior seemed to say to him, "Shall I spare your child? Will you retain her, or suffer her to come unto me?" His heart replied, "Thou knowest, Lord, how my life is in the child; yet I can not say, 'Restore her,' for I can not have *my will* done. Not as *I* will, but as *thou* wilt." And this was the habitual way in which his will acted. So it should be with all Christians; so it may be, and so we trust it often is.

As to the Intellect, we may surely hope to attain a

knowledge of the will of God concerning us, so as to be able, intelligently, to perform it. Our character lies in the *end* which we choose and for which we live, and the law of God reveals, and Christ's life illustrates, what this end should be; and, doubtless, the Holy Ghost will so bring this home to our apprehension, that we can become, and remain, consciously devoted to it, and that we may know our specific acts to be in harmony with it and executive of it.

It does not seem clear that we are to expect or wait for a special revelation of the will of God in respect to each one of our *specific acts*. If our *end* is right, our *spirit*, Christ-like, God may naturally leave us to learn, by the powers he has given us, what our *particular acts* ought to be. Indeed, he may be indifferent which of several courses we take to accomplish a benevolent end, and his blessing may equally follow upon either of several feasible methods. This is the way we deal with our children. Having prepared them by careful instruction, and secured an obedient spirit, we give them their choice in modes of action, we throw them upon their individual resources, and prefer to have them exercise their own powers, that they may gain confidence, discipline, and strength. We do not cramp their faculties by forbidding them to take a step till we shall have given them specific directions how and where to step. We encourage them to act on their own judgment. If there be occasion, we direct them specifically; and where they lack wisdom, we give it to them. Is it not so between God and his children? He has given us reason and his word to guide us. If we lack wisdom, he promises to give liberally. And, certainly, he would have us learn so to use the faculties with which he has endowed us as to gain character and strength as independent moral beings. Is there not, then, a margin for the exercise of our own powers? and may not the true disciple hear his Father saying, "My child, your aim is right — my love constrains you. Now use your best judgment with the light you have; throw yourself upon your powers made in my likeness, and act as seems to you best, and I shall be equally well pleased whichever of the several possible ways you take. You will gain strength by the use of your faculties, and suffer loss by their disuse. If you make a mistake, be not troubled. But learn wisdom. Ask for light when you need it, and it shall not be withheld. Be a man. Fear not. Keep your heart in my love, and all shall be well."

Different disciples, with the same end in view, constrained by the same love, do, we know, choose different methods of working, according to their varying temperaments and capacities of judging.

The theory here stated, therefore, seems more consistent with the Bible, with reason, and with facts, than the theory of the author of "Millennial Experience," who seems to teach that we are to be guided in each specific act of life — even the smallest — by a direct revelation, to the mind, of the will of God.

An illustration of the principle above stated, that God is pleased with our independent use of our capabilities, occurs to mind. An intelligent young man found himself pressed to the performance of an important duty. But there were two ways of doing it, and he had long halted between them. Some insist that there is only one way; others, that either of two or three will answer as well before God. He had determined to settle the question of *how*, and act. He read the books on either side; and the more he read, the more confused he became, till he despaired, "by searching," of being able to decide. He came to me for advice. I asked, "Are you willing to take either course? Is your own will submissive, so that, the moment the path is opened, you will enter it?" He believed it was. "Go, then," I said, "and so report to your Savior, and ask for orders." He went, and almost immediately received this answer: "Take which course you please; your Heavenly Father does not care which." The answer was as clear as his clearest religious experience, and his trouble was all over. He acted upon his own good sense, and had abundant reason to be satisfied with the course he had taken.

But much more, *as to the Intellect*, may be attained, than the mere knowledge of God's will concerning us. As shown in previous sections, we may know God himself. We may have his thoughts, his ideas, his views filling and perfectly satisfying the intelligence. The knowledge of God, setting, as it does, all other knowledge in its proper adjustments, is the highest and best the universe affords. Many, alas, are slow in coming to this knowledge; many things have to be learned through severe processes of discipline; yet, if a man will search for it as for hid treasures, his intellect shall become as the garden of the Lord, full of all delights, and redolent of the aroma of heaven.

As to the Sensibility, we may well hope to gain that "peace of God which passeth all understanding." The lowest degree of attainment should bring us an experience so satisfying, in kind, that we shall only be hungry for more of that which gives us present blessedness. This holy and happy satisfaction may become so deep that surface agitation will in no wise destroy our peace. It is quite possible to *enjoy* trials, to *glory* in tribulation, to *take pleasure* in suffering for the name of the Lord Jesus. When the Holy Spirit exhibits to the soul the fullness of its inheritance, its blessedness, like the love of God, "passeth knowledge," and the forms of language are insufficient to crystallize it into expression. Admitting the fact of more or less irritation of the sensibility by the pressure of temptation and wrong, especially in natures constructed of over-sensitive or inflexible materials, yet the earnest Christian may hope to attain to a deep under-current of ever-increasing blessedness, beautifully illustrated by Ezekiel (47 : 1–12). The stream is small at first, as it issues from under the temple, and flows around by the altar; but it passes on a thousand cubits, and the water is up to the ankles; another thousand, and it is up to the knees; another thousand, and the waters are up to the loins; another thousand, and the river is deep and broad, and can not be crossed. This river carried life in its waters, even to the "healing of the sea," whither it flowed, and to all things therein. Of this stream, David speaks (Ps. 46) : "There is a river, the streams whereof shall make glad the city of God, the holy place of the tabernacles of the Most High." The same stream waters the New Jerusalem. On its borders, it is appointed unto the Israel of God to dwell, amid living trees perfecting their rich clusters continually, and scattering their leaves for the healing of the nations.

When we consider that our Lord may take his trustful disciple up into his own moral atmosphere, where the "light is dry and pure," and, from his own point of observation, give him to see in that light of which the sun is but a dim shadow; that he may turn all his works, as seen through microscope and telescope, and all the sciences with their wonderful revealings, into a vast system of reflectors, symbols, and illustrations, interpreting himself to us; that, in each event of our individual experience and history, and in all the unfoldings of his providence, and in the startling changes in the history of the nations, he may distinctly show us his own hand, working out the good pleasure of his will in the redemption of his church, — we may indeed conclude that no limit can be set to what our God may do for us, even while we remain in the flesh.

Section X.

The Relation of Faith to the Obtaining of this Saving Knowledge of God.

We have, in a former chapter, given a brief analysis of saving faith. In such faith, it appears that the *will* grasps and enthrones the *object* of faith, namely, God and his truth, as far as apprehended by the intelligence, and makes it the law of life. In a dead faith, on the other hand, while God and the truth are more or less clearly revealed to the knowing power, the *will refuses* to fall in with that truth and *enthrone* it as the mind's law.

Faith, then, is the grand indispensable *condition* of our salvation, at every step of its progress. To believe, in the true sense, is to open the door to Christ, and to welcome all saving influences to practical supremacy in the soul. It connects the branch with the living vine, and admits God, and the whole power of the gospel, into vital and working contact with the soul. It is the link which couples the car to the engine — the soul to God. It opens the valve for the steam to enter and act upon the mental and moral machinery. Not to believe, in the sense defined, is really to reject the gospel, to resist the Holy Ghost, and make the truth of God of none effect. It excludes all redeeming agencies from the mind, and practically abandons the soul to the ruin which sin involves. It forecloses the intellect, pre-occupies the sensibility, perverts the will, and resigns the throne to the adversary.

Great care must be taken not to substitute untruths, our fancies, speculations, or theories, in the place of the truth which alone is the power of God unto salvation. We have shown, in Chapter VI., the importance of the right adjustment of the will; and it is nowhere more essential than in our faith. Not unfrequently, the mistake is made of accepting some vivid conception or picture of a religious "experience" as the object of faith. When this is done, all the powers of the mind are put upon the stretch *to realize such an experience.* But the effort fails, of course. This "picture" takes the place before the mind which belongs to God and his word. No man may take the exercises of another, and expect the Spirit to lead him in the same precise way. The Infinite One is original in all his working. We must submit our ideals to him, and welcome his hand to mold our clay as seemeth him good. Our faith must not stand either in the wisdom or the *experience* of men, but in the promises and power of God. If we would have light, we should look at the sun itself, not merely at some object on which it has shone.

Section XI.

The Duty of Living in the Victorious Enjoyment of this Life-sustaining Knowledge of God.

Duty is a sacred word. It is what we *owe* — what is *due* from us to ourselves or others.

"The wish, the dream, the wild desire, *to know*," is not only the highest, but the truest impulse of man's intellectual being. It is duty as well as privilege. The knowledge of God, crowning and setting all other knowledge in its true relations, ought, of course, to be the chief object of pursuit. On its acquisition, all our true interests — our success or failure as moral beings — depend.

We owe it to our Savior to attain to that full knowledge of him which will insure us a triumphant and habitual victory over "the world, the flesh, and the devil." The most intimate fellowship with valued friends is the spontaneous bidding of affection. Jesus Christ is our infinite Friend. No other has loved us with a love like his. When there was no eye to pity and no arm to save, he said unto us, "Live." We know all the story of his sufferings in our behalf, and how he gives himself to us as Mediator, Intercessor, Advocate, Bridegroom, and in all loving offices.

Surely that wondrous benevolence by which he not only supplies the want of every living thing, but gives himself to the death of the cross, that so he may lift the whole race up into the sphere of his own blessedness, with special manifestations of sympathy for the poor and needy, throws upon all men, but especially upon his children, an immeasurable obligation to catch the spirit of the apostle, and know nothing but Christ and him crucified; to suffer the loss of all things, that they may attain the fullness of that knowledge, and be forever "complete in Him" who is "over all, God blessed forever."

If we seek not to know Christ as our ever-present and almighty Deliverer, we shall inevitably abuse and dishonor him at every step. Our experience will correspond with that of the disciples before the day of Pentecost. Like Peter, we shall deny him; like Thomas, distrust him; like them all, we shall forsake him, and sink under the pressure of temptation. The "power of the resurrection" we can not know, and our Redeemer will practically be to us, as he was for a little time to the disciples, as one dead in the hands of his enemies. Even our past experience will lose its significance, and we shall be as much bewildered as were the two whom Jesus met on their way to Emmaus. If we do not so know him, all our Christian graces will be dwarfed. Our love, our faith, our joy can rise no higher than our apprehension of him. We can not enter fully into sympathy with him in that work which thrills every holy heart in glory; we can not truly represent his spirit or his will to the world; our light will be but darkness. If we do not go on so to know him, we shall fail of the work and fruits of the Spirit; for he accomplishes his mission by the manifestation of the knowledge of God.

We owe it to the church of Christ to be full of this victorious knowledge. His church suffers, — "the boar out of the wood doth waste it, and the wild beast of the field doth devour it" (Ps. 80 : 13), — and, by reflecting upon her the light of such spiritual attainment, we can do much to "make her wilderness like Eden, and her desert like the garden of the Lord."

We owe it as well to a lost world. Sinners are perishing. We can successfully point them, by such knowledge, to the "Lamb of God who taketh away the sin of the world."

We owe it not less to ourselves. Only by so doing can we fulfill the mission God has given us. Why should we suffer unbelief and selfishness to reign over us, and mar the image of God in our natures, when deliverance is possible? Why be the bond slaves of Satan, since Jesus has purchased and proclaimed liberty?

Section XII.

The Guilt of being without this Knowledge and its Saving Power.

Many will think themselves sorry that they have not this saving knowledge, and be ready, perhaps, to find fault with God that he has withheld it from them, so that they have seemed unable to perform the duty already urged. But, alas! their ignorance is their sin.

According to the apostle (Rom. 1:28), God gives men up to sin and darkness only because they are "unwilling to retain him in their knowledge." God surely has done his utmost to persuade men to come and take freely the life-giving waters. The conditions are easy. "If any man will do his will, he shall know of the doctrine." If men will search for it as for earthly treasure, they " shall find the knowledge of God."

What has not God done to make himself known to the world? Before our first parents had left the garden, he began to reveal himself in mercy. All along the track of history, he has erected monuments to indicate his character to his creatures. What a testimony to his hatred of sin was the deluge! In all his dealings with the Jewish nation, God was working out, for the instruction of all generations, his views of sin and holiness. He has spoken his will by holy men, and given their utterances miraculous confirmation.

*In due time came the Incarnation — God manifest in the flesh. This coming of the Messiah in a human form, addressing himself to all our senses, putting himself into our conditions that he might give the fullest expression to the loving heart of God toward us, by voice, by act, by visible sympathy, was the highest possible manifestation he could make of himself in the world of sense. It brought the knowledge of God to the level of the lowest man.

Then, the story of the Messiah, with all his revealings, was put on record, and carefully preserved, and handed down from generation to generation, that all might know and live.

Then, as the culmination of effort on God's part, to make himself savingly known, he sends his Holy Spirit upon the one great mission of seizing upon all the unfoldings of the divine character from Eden to Calvary, and of presenting them before men in such a way that, seeing them, they should be constrained to believe and become partakers of his moral life.

The Spirit is sent on this mission to every man; and God testifies that he is more willing to bestow the Spirit upon all who are willing to receive it, than earthly parents are to give good gifts to their children.

His great, crowning, and most glorious promise to his people is, that he will send them the Holy Spirit to dwell permanently with them in the world, to be their Comforter, Teacher, and Sanctifier. He shall take of the things of Jesus and show them to them; he shall bring all things to their remembrance; he shall sanctify and seal them through the truth unto their becoming partakers of the divine nature, and overcoming the corruption that is in the world through lust.

Nothing remains, therefore, for the disciples of Christ, but *to believe* and receive this saving, triumphant knowledge of God. Does it not even appear that, if we fail, it must be because of unbelief and of resistance to the Holy Ghost himself?

May I not, in concluding the presentation of this topic, urge my readers, and especially those who have "the beginning of confidence," to drop all excuses and misgivings, and come boldly to Jesus for this higher knowledge of himself? He "hangs out the white flag;" he presents the "golden scepter" to all who would approach him. If the soul is poor, he has gold to enrich it; if wounded and sick, balm to heal it. The feast is ready; the door is open. Come with a will; wrench the soul from all the falsehoods of Satan, and accept of Jesus as All.

Section XIII.

The General View here presented, confirmed by its Power to harmonize the apparently Conflicting Views of the Different Schools of Evangelical Christians, and to simplify certain Vexed Questions in Theology.

If one were putting together a dissected map, and found the part in hand exactly fitted to all the surrounding parts, so that the lines and words on the face perfectly corresponded, he would be sure he was, so far, right. On the same principle, if the doctrines of this book, and especially of this chapter, should be found to match in with the great surrounding truths of the Bible, that would go far to establish their truth. If they should prove to be a key, by which a beautiful and substantial harmony should be disclosed between what seem to be conflicting views of different denominations of Evangelical Christians, this would further tend to confirm them, and make their presentation alike agreeable and profitable to all such Christians.

We wish modestly to suggest, whether, in several respects, they may not be regarded as such a key.

In the discussion of the question of entire sanctification in this life, one class of Christians has insisted, and another denied, that the Bible taught that doctrine. Each supports its view from the Scriptures.

Now, where does the truth lie? or is it true, as cavilers say, that you can prove or disprove any thing from the Word of God?

The Bible plainly recognizes those who are in Christ as being, in some sense, "holy," "clean," "obedient." Our Lord, in speaking of his disciples before his death, says, "Now ye are *clean* through the word which I have spoken unto you." And again, he says to the Father, "I have given unto them the words which thou gavest me, and they have received them, *and have kept them.*" Paul, in his third chapter to the Philippians, recognizes Christians as both perfect and imperfect. He urges "as many as be perfect" to press on to a perfection which he was striving to reach, but had not yet attained. He appeals to the Thessalonians, ten years before, that they, and God also, knew how "holily, and justly, and unblamably" he had deported himself among them; and yet he frequently represents himself as the weakest and most unworthy of all, and as struggling against temptation, and as laboring to attain a yet higher spiritual position.

At the time Christ declared his disciples to be clean and obedient to the word, they were, nevertheless, so weak, and, in some sense, so imperfect, that in "that hour" of trial which was just before them, they all forsook the Master and fled,—Peter denying him with oaths and curses.

Now, according to the view we have taken, these

disciples had some knowledge of God by the Spirit — enough to make them accepted followers of Christ. To this knowledge they were obedient, and, in this sense, clean. At the same time, they were ignorant of the things, the knowledge of which by the Spirit, would have saved them from falling. Had they known, *then*, what was revealed to them on the day of Pentecost, and what it was, perhaps, impossible for them so to know sooner, it is morally certain they would not have fallen. They would have been as unshaken in that most fearful crisis of human trial, as they were subsequently, when filled with the Holy Ghost. But while the Shepherd was smitten, the sheep would almost unavoidably, and for the moment, be scattered. The remedy which alone would have kept them, was to be developed out of this very smiting of the Shepherd.

The sense in which the disciples were holy and clean before the day of Pentecost, is obvious. They walked according to all the light which had really penetrated their consciousness at the time. Being in Christ, his righteousness was theirs. Their sin was all pardoned, and no condemnation from heaven rested upon them. If virtue is an intelligible thing; if it consists in a whole-hearted, voluntary obedience to the known will of God; and if the knowledge of God is only attainable by degrees, — then holiness is a thing of degrees, and the disciples were, in some sense, holy before the day of Pentecost as really as after that day. It is a precious fact, that the true disciple, though but a babe, is fully and perfectly justified before the Father. The law shall lay nothing to his charge. He is in Christ, and is as perfectly accepted now, while conformed to the light which belongs to his spiritual infancy, as he will be when his knowledge and corresponding obedience shall have carried him up to his spiritual manhood. Of course, all boasting is excluded alike at every stage of attainment, for all is of grace. Boasting is a fruit of self-righteousness alone, not of that which is of God by faith.

On the theory we have presented, the harmony of the Bible is apparent. There is a substantial sense in which the Christian who walks fully up to the knowledge he has attained, is holy, clean, obedient; and another, not inconsistent sense, in which, lacking higher knowledge from the Spirit, and the consequent completeness of strength and usefulness it would give him, he is yet imperfect as a Christian, and has need to heed the injunction and example of Paul, and press on toward the highest attainments in the knowledge and life of God, growing in grace and wisdom, and in favor with God and man.

Again: the two apparently conflicting theories, that sanctification is an instantaneous, and that it is a progressive work, are, by our view, harmonized. The revelation of knowledge, the manifestation of truth to the mind by the Spirit, as on the day of

Pentecost, is often instantaneous; and so far as sanctification is effected by this inflowing of divine knowledge, it must be an instantaneous work.

But, on the other hand, the Spirit shows us the things of Christ as we are able to receive them, after long inquiry and study often, one at a time, one thing to-day, and another to-morrow, and so on forever; and for that reason, sanctification, as the result of advancing knowledge, must be a progressive work, advancing in depth and power as divine knowledge increases.

Again: according to the theory of some, there remains in the Christian heart, after conversion, what is termed, in the somewhat blind language of theology, much "inbred corruption," which sanctification is supposed to remove. Does not the view we have presented give an intelligible idea of what this "inbred corruption" is, and how it is to be removed? Was not the "inbred corruption" of the disciples between their conversion and their sanctification, so to call it, on the day of Pentecost, simply that working of their minds according to nature and habit which was consequent on their having, as yet, so little and such imperfect knowledge of God and Christ by the Holy Ghost? And was not its removal, the natural result to them of the divine manifestation they received on the day of the Spirit's advent?

Again: the apparently conflicting doctrines of "ability" and "inability" may, in the light of our theory, be seen to be perfectly true and harmonious.

The will is, in its nature, free, and all moral action involves choice. God requires men to choose, to will, as he does. But there are some absolute conditions to the exercise of choice. There must be an object of choice, and this object must be made known to the mind. God himself, in his will and character, is the proper object of choice; but he can not be truly and intelligently chosen until he is made known to us by his Spirit, who alone can reveal him. The use of our ability to love and obey God, depends, then, absolutely upon him. A man who is lost may have ability to go home, but he can not use it till he knows which way to go: his difficulty is not want of ability directly, but of knowledge. Does not the old school doctrine of inability lie exactly here, and is it not true? But when an object, worthy of choice or love, is revealed to the mind's apprehension, then we can easily and naturally bring our ability into play, and choose it. We can take hold upon it, and receive it into our hearts. This we are doing every day. Does not the new school doctrine of ability lie here, and is it not true, and beautifully harmonious with the doctrine of apparent inability?

"Man lost all ability of will in the fall," says the Catechism, to love and obey God. And was it not, because he thereby lost the knowledge of God, and, according to Paul (Eph. 4:18), became "alienated from the life of God through the ignorance of him" which sin involved, that he lost his ability to love and serve God? To lose the knowledge of God is, practically, so far, to lose our ability to love him.

Both schools say, nevertheless, that no man is excusable for remaining in sin. And does not the reason for this lie in the fact that God has put *some* knowledge of himself in every man's reason, and set it forth in his works, so that all may lay hold of that, and be led on, from step to step, in the advancing light of providence, and grace, and revelation, unto eternal life? Free as the will is, we are still dependent on the Spirit for a knowledge of the true object to be chosen; but the Holy One knows this, and waits to be gracious. The Sun of Righteousness shines all about us, and his light is shut out from men's minds only by a positive volition closing the eyes against it.

The Bible is entirely consistent in holding men under obligation immediately to obey God, and in teaching that no man can come unto him except he is drawn by the Holy Spirit. The conditions of choice, so far as they are dependent upon God, are fulfilled; obligation is complete. The new school teacher need not fear to press men at once to lay hold of an offered Savior, to rush into Mercy's outstretched arms, through any apprehension that the Spirit's part of the work will not be performed; nor need the old school divine embarrass his efforts by the consideration of the sinner's inability. Let him summon the transgressor to an immediate surrender to a loving and waiting Savior.

Again: the two apparently opposite doctrines of the sinfulness and non-sinfulness of our nature may, perhaps, receive some hopeful elucidation from our theory.

If you put *falsehood*, instead of *truth*, into the intellect; if the "law of sin," of supreme selfishness, be the thing known there and held as *true*, and if the will is given up and committed to the execution, in life, of this law so enthroned in the mind, then, of course, and by its very nature and constitution, the whole mental and moral machinery will go wrong, invariably so. The thinking, the feeling, the acting, whether it be "plowing" or praying, will be all sinful and out of the way. Depravity, in one form or another, must and will be the outcome. If you reverse the action of the machinery, the locomotive will only go backward on or off the track, and down the embankment, or wherever the switch and rails will let it go. Adjust the machinery properly, and it will do its work all right. It is in the nature of the machinery so to act in the one case, and, by the same law, contrariwise in the other. So with the mind, when its action is reversed by the consecration of the will to falsehood, held as truth in the understanding. It is a thing of course, and the mind can not act otherwise than wrong under these conditions. It will go backward from God and rectitude, speaking lies and doing whatever the enthroned law of selfishness demands. On the other hand, adjust the will to the truth, and, by the laws of its being, in this case as in the other, the action of the mind will correspond with the truth. By his very nature, then, when a man so perverts his powers, he is wholly sinful, totally depraved.

Since God has done the best that possibly could be done for moral agents to lead them not to reverse the action of their powers, but to operate them according to *truth* as he has revealed and will reveal it, and since the only reason why men have not the knowledge of God — even the heathen — is, that they are "unwilling to retain" it in their hearts, his ways need no vindication, and we can not excuse our sins on the supposition of a sinful nature. A nature which would work in opposite moral directions — forward or backward, toward good or evil — in accordance with his sovereign choice of truth or falsehood is the glorious prerogative of a free moral agent.

Does not, then, the relation of the mind's willful knowledge or ignorance of God to its practical working, help to solve the difficulty of a so-called sinful nature? If such a relation, as our theory suggests, exists, — if men, to be moral agents, must have natures capable of development under laws of error as well as of truth, of evil as well as of good, — why find fault with God for giving us such natures, or why look back into a pre-existent state for a method of justifying God in his dealings with the race?

Again: one class of Christians say, that to be in doubt and great uncertainty about our acceptance with Christ, and about the genuineness of our religious exercises, is a better evidence of our good estate than to be confident and firmly assured. Another class hold the opposite view, and say, that to doubt is wrong; that confidence and full assurance are to be expected and cherished. The former class are annoyed by the exulting and positive experience of the latter; and the latter class pity and blame the former for their apparent lack of confidence and joyful assurance in the infinitely trustworthy and glorious Savior. Where does the truth lie? Or has each view its element of truth?

We answer, that to doubt and distrust the testimony of God's Spirit, to receive with suspicion and misgivings the knowledge which he gives, is clearly wrong, and must be of evil tendency. If *he* testifies to our spirits, and bears his witness (Rom. 8: 16), that we are the children of God, and if *he* put the "Abba, Father," into our hearts, then to doubt and distrust is to treat him as a liar! If the testimony of God may not give assurance, then assurance is impossible, and universal unbelief and skepticism are inevitable. Ought Abraham to have admitted doubt into his mind during those twenty-five long years, while he was waiting for the fulfillment of the promise? Paul commends his faith as an example to the whole Israel of God, for the express reason that he refused to "stagger," and persisted, with "full persuasion," in the faithfulness of God, although the temptation to doubt was such as compelled him to "hope against hope." When Peter could say in the very presence of Christ, "Lord, thou knowest all things; thou knowest that I love thee," ought he to have doubted his acceptance? When Paul was conscious to himself that he "counted all things but loss for the excellency of the knowledge of Christ," and that he was unwilling to know any thing but Christ and him crucified, ought he to have distrusted his acceptance, and accounted his *doubts* the best evidence that his name was in the book of life? When Luther heard the Holy Ghost say to his toiling, self-righteous soul, "The just shall live by faith," should he have doubted? Ought any man who has been earnestly inquiring the way of life, and who has, consciously, as a lost sinner, cast himself trustfully upon the Savior of lost sinners, and who has found his broken heart and subdued will, saying, "Lord, what wilt thou have me to do?" and sweetly preferring the will of Jesus above all else, — ought he to doubt, or should he boldly "reckon himself" an accepted disciple of Christ? Nothing would suit Satan better, or enable him to cripple the elect of God more effectually, than that, in such circumstances, they should yield to doubt, and thus distrust the testimony of the Holy Ghost. The Bible, every where, aims to produce the most unwavering confidence toward God.

But if we attempt to prove to ourselves our discipleship on any other testimony than that of the Spirit and Word of God, or by any testimony the natural man can furnish, or by any proof drawn from our own works of righteousness, we may well be full of doubt and uncertainty. To doubt *such* testimony *is* better evidence of piety than to give it full credit.

But will not both classes of Christians referred to be found to agree perfectly in cherishing the fullest confidence in all the knowledge of God and of our own spiritual states which the Holy Ghost shall attest, and agree in maintaining the utter untrustworthiness of any conclusions concerning the things of the Spirit which are not verified by his testimony? While God will not lie, and can not be mistaken, it is certain that a selfish heart is sure to be mistaken about divine things. We may, therefore, trust God implicitly, and yet "have no confidence in the flesh."

Again: there is a difference among Christians as to the means of attaining to a state of practical sanctification in the world. Some would set forth the abstract idea of holiness, and urge men to seek it directly by an act of faith, and to profess its attainment as a means of retaining the blessing. Others have no hope of being able to reach such a spiritual state by any direct effort to gain it, or to help the matter by professing its attainment. Their idea is, faithfully to perform their duty, and leave their sanctification to be wrought out for them by the Spirit, without any agency of their own.

Now, if the view we have set forth is the true one, it is not a state of sanctification which is to be sought after and obtained by an act of faith *directly*, but the *knowledge of God by the Spirit*, the result of which is, a degree of sanctification answering in measure to the knowledge gained. What we are called upon to profess, or testify to, for the honor of God and for the encouragement of others, is, that *which we have learned of him*, with grateful recognition of its effects upon our own hearts and lives. Those who ignore any effort to gain the great spiritual victory designated by the term " sanctification," or " assurance of faith," overlook the palpable fact that the " knowledge of God " is promised only to those who seek for it with all the heart; and that, although the blessing was specially promised, by the ascending Redeemer, within a few days, the disciples did nevertheless assemble in an upper room, and there wait in prayer and supplication, with one accord, till, on the day of Pentecost, the blessing came. We once heard a distinguished clergyman condemn special prayer meetings to pray for the baptism of the Spirit, on the ground that the blessing was only to be gained as the result of earnest activity in the performance of religious duty.

If he meant to say that the reflex influence upon the mind of duty performed is identical with the Spirit's baptism, or that the gift of the Spirit is procured by works and not by faith, was he not in manifest error? If he meant to intimate that, for those who perform their known duty, such gatherings and such waiting upon God for the blessing are out of place, was he not in error? If he meant to condemn praying for the manifestation of the Spirit, on the part of those who refuse to perform their known duty, if there be such, his strictures were plainly not amiss. All parties should harmonize in the determination, first, to do all the known will of God, and then to wait on God, "with all prayer and supplication," "without ceasing," with the faith of an Abraham and the urgency of a Jacob, for that promised work of the Spirit, which, from glory to glory, shall develop the soul into the image of Christ

CHAPTER XXVI.

SATAN'S METHODS OF OPPOSING THE CHRISTIAN'S SANCTIFICATION.

Now, the serpent was more subtle than any beast of the field which the Lord God had made.— Gen. 3: 1.

ALL that has been said in previous chapters of the devices of Satan, applies here. In all the methods hitherto pointed out, the adversary opposes the progress of the church in a holy life; and he does it with increased subtlety as she presses her way upward into the higher spheres of religious truth and experience.

As we have abundantly shown, all advancement in holiness is the fruit of the Spirit, acquainting the soul with God. To make progress, the believer must needs maintain the right attitude of mind toward the Sanctifier. In the words of the apostle, he must be "led by the Spirit," and "walk in the Spirit." To prevent his doing this, Satan will do his utmost. When he can not successfully deny to men the existence of the Holy Ghost, he will insinuate doubts as to the possibility of being taught by an invisible, disembodied being,— at least, suggest grave difficulties in the way; he will provoke self-will, and pride, and an unteachable spirit, and make men forget their

24*

dependence, and "lean to their own understandings;" he will himself counterfeit the work of the Comforter, and infuse his own subtle and plausible suggestions to counteract the Spirit's ministrations, and nullify all his teachings.

After a man has gained so much knowledge of God as is implied in becoming a Christian, and has learned the beginnings of gospel truth, the effort of Satan will be to prevent his continuing firmly obedient to this knowledge. In this way, he often entirely arrests the soul's progress. The believer, having entered upon the Christian course, must be subjected to the refining process by pruning-knife, or crucible, or cross; and the question at issue will be, whether he will obey the truth and follow Christ, when the soul is overwhelmed with "heaviness through manifold temptations," or resist and turn back? Not unfrequently, in such conflict, Satan bewilders and baffles the Christian, and gains a temporary advantage, carrying the will over even to the denial of the Master. Happy will it be for one thus overcome, if, like Peter, he shall go out and weep bitterly, and so, immediately find himself re-united to Christ in a more firm and loving obedience.

Satan, again, will strive hard to satisfy the mind with a mere natural apprehension of divine things, instead of that knowledge of them which it is the sole province of the Holy Ghost to give. Such knowledge can bring no life. How many, alas! know

Christ only by hearsay! They have read of him in the Bible, heard eloquent discourses about him from the pulpit, have seen his portrait; but they have never "beheld the Lamb of God," by the Spirit's showing, so as to have their sins "taken away." They are "ever learning" about Christ and his doctrine in the light of their own beclouded powers, but are "never able to come to the knowledge of the truth" in its sanctifying efficacy.

Again: Satan will, if possible, awaken a practical unbelief in respect to the feasibility of living a triumphantly victorious life while in the flesh. How few persons really expect, habitually, to overcome the world! They know they are to be tempted, and believe the tempter will triumph over them. They magnify the power of the adversary, they dwell upon the peculiar difficulties of their case, and are afraid to venture upon the Deliverer with a full confidence that he will make them conquerors indeed, by his own power. They fear to make the promises their own; they forget the covenant and the oath of the Redeemer; they lose sight of the "strongholds," — the altar and the mercy-seat, — and have no heart to insist, "*By these the victory is mine, now and forever.*" Thus they are full of a subtle unbelief, into which Satan has inveigled them. They have bowed their necks to the yoke of bondage, which they expect to wear all their lives, looking to their own death, at last, for deliverance, instead of looking now to Christ for a power to break their yoke, and to put them into "the glorious liberty of the children of God." So unbelieving has the church been, that it has often been deemed almost a heresy to hold that a practical victory over " the world, the flesh, and the devil," is even possible to the Christian.

So long as Satan is allowed to hold the mind in such a form of unbelief as this, no real progress can be made in the divine life. There will be no earnest "fighting of the good fight of faith;" or if it be attempted, defeat will only succeed defeat; for " this is the victory that overcometh the world, even our faith."

Again: it will be like Satan to awaken prejudice against the doctrine of sanctification, as he did against the Lord Jesus Christ, so that men will be repelled from inquiring after the truth. It will be another similar device of the adversary, to give men a perverted view of the doctrine, to make it seem incomprehensible, or mystical, or impracticable, and thus to render it of none effect.

Again: Satan will take great pains to conceal from men the marvelous simplicity of the way of holiness. Salvation is all a free gift, without money or price. God is the GREAT GIVER. He *gives* every thing, and with a bountifulness corresponding to his infinite nature. There can be no traffic between us and God. Our exchanges with him must all be made, not on the principle of debt and credit, loss and gain, but of giving and receiving. He gives us every thing with himself, and we must give all to him — give it to him out and out — not for a price, not for heaven even, nor for salvation, nor for any other equivalent. His gifts and ours are not equal at all, nor does he require them to be. His are infinite; ours are nothing and less than nothing to him. The higher blessings of the gospel, equally with the lower, are the simple *gifts* of God. Now, Satan seeks to hide all this from the mind, and to set men, upon commercial principles, to buying salvation, to proposing an equivalent for it. Said a gentleman to his wife, who had found Jesus as a full and present Savior, "My dear, how did you get this blessing? what did you do to obtain it?" "I did not do any thing; God *gave* it to me." This opened his eyes. He was toiling and struggling to gain it, as a man struggles to make money, to gain earthly good; as Luther was working, when God said to him, "The just shall live by faith." It was a new idea to him that the Infinite Giver *had* given, even to him, eternal life (1 John 5 : 11), and that he had only to accept it, — to *believe* the record which God had made, — to secure the blessing in his own soul. He did believe, and his heart, too, was satisfied. Salvation, from beginning to end, is free to every humble, trusting applicant. It can not be had for a price, whether it be the money offered by Simon Magus, or the good works gloried in by the Pharisee. Let not Satan blind the reader, then, to the simplicity of the way. *God has given us every thing;* believe it; prove him. Let your intercourse with him be all on the principle of love; let there be the perpetual exchange of gifts. *Give him all you have* — yourself, your love, your confidence, your obedience, your name, influence, fortune, friends; *give all,* ALL, ALL; and take gratefully *his gifts* to you — his Son, his Spirit, his promises, the heavenly inheritance — the "all things" which he has said "are yours." Let his gifts interpret to you his love; and let that love work in you a responsive, all-consuming love to him; and let the free gift to him of your whole being express and illustrate your devotion to his will.

Again: Satan will persuade men that it is not necessary to make special attainments in holiness in this life. He can suggest, "You have been converted; your name is in the book of life; the doctrine of the saints' perseverance is true, and you will not fail of heaven; you will become holy when you die, and this is all-sufficient." To listen, for a moment, to such a suggestion, is unworthy of a disciple of Christ. The Scriptures demand growth in grace, and would inspire us to leave the things that are behind, and to go on toward spiritual maturity and manhood, and to be steadfast in obedience to Christ. They require this as positively as they require the first acts of submission and repentance for sin. Our usefulness, our mission in the world, demand that we "go forward," though the sea and the wilderness are before us. We must advance and overcome the world, or be overcome by it, and fall back into a life of sin and unbelief, in which we shall "forget that we were purged from our old sins," and they will return, with a sevenfold strength, to bring us again in bondage.

Many, again, are kept from special and rapid progress in the divine life, by the wrong public sentiment and the unfavorable example which prevail in the churches. In some churches the tendency is strong in the direction of conformity to the world, and of a loose liberality in sentiment. It is not difficult for Satan to persuade men to measure themselves by themselves, and to compare themselves among themselves, and thus to satisfy them with an almost ruinous standard of attainment.

Again: the grand device of Satan to prevent the sanctification of the church will be, of course, to hold the mind in a state of self-righteousness, as a means of keeping it from the "righteousness which is of God by faith;" to confuse and reverse, in men's experiences, the principles of faith and works. The urgency with which Paul treated this subject shows that he regarded it as Satan's stronghold.

What, definitely, is *self*-righteousness? That man is *self*-righteous, who, feeling the natural sense of obligation to do right, and taking his idea of what *is* right from his own darkened mind or from the letter of the Bible, tries, by the energy he has within him by nature, to bring his voluntary acts into conformity with this idea. Now, by such "deeds of the law" no man can be justified; and for two reasons: (1.) His idea is wrong. He makes righteousness to consist in specific, and generally outward acts, while the right thing which God requires is a state of mind — a supreme *love* to him and equal love to men. (2.) Men are not, as a matter of fact, successful in carrying into execution that which they know, in reason, to be right. Their supreme selfishness effectually counteracts their subordinate purpose to do right. It so perverts their judgment and conscience, that what their selfishness dictates they call right, and, therefore, often do the most wicked things under the notion that they are righteous. The Jews did this of old; men have done so in all ages. The dominant law of sin and selfishness, which reigns in all unregenerate men, often so crushes out the impulse of natural affection, even, and overrules all the better sentiments of human nature, that father is arrayed against son, and son against father, and brother against brother, in the most angry and bloody strife, each insisting that he is doing right. Of course, only *self*-righteousness exists in such cases. The righteousness which is of God by faith never wars against itself, nor against the divinely implanted qualities of our natures.

The universal consciousness and experience of the

race is, that man's powers are so weakened by sin, that he can not be trusted to do right under the pressure of temptation, even though he should seem determined to do so. We will not hear the testimony of an interested witness, nor suffer him upon the juror's bench. He will not withstand the cataract of temptation; his selfishness, not his unperverted sense of right, will rule over him; and how then can he be acquitted at the bar of eternal justice?

Self-righteous men fail to understand the true character of God, and to take into proper account their relations to him, and his claims upon them. Suppose the prodigal, in the land of his estrangement, had said to himself, "I will be a gentleman, a good, honest citizen, pay my debts, and conform to the moral maxims of the people:" he might have passed for a righteous man among his neighbors; but would that have reconciled matters between him and his father? Mr. Jefferson Davis may be the fairest of men before his fellow-secessionists; he may be a model of honor before foreign powers whose aid he seeks in his rebellion; he may proclaim fasts and petition Heaven with urgent supplications for help in his wild crusade; he may even have deceived himself into the idea that he is doing right; but would all this help his standing with the United Sates government, to which a hundred oaths of allegiance have bound him, all of which he has broken? How absurd to expect he could be justified and acquitted by our

Supreme Court, on the ground that his present acts of war on this government, which he calls right acts, are so in fact! Is it not infinitely more absurd to think that a sinner in rebellion against God can be justified, in the Supreme Court of Heaven, on the ground that his so-called right acts are in accordance with God's holy law, and are, therefore, acceptable to him in the place of a heart of loyal and loving obedience? Nothing but condemnation can possibly await the mere moralist at the bar of eternal justice!

What, on the other hand, is the righteousness of God by faith? It begins in the confession that we are utterly lost and condemned by the law, and that no acts of ours, while the heart itself remains alienated from God, can be acceptable to him and conformed to his requirements. Despairing of justification by any merits of our own, we betake ourselves, in penitence and faith, to Christ, the sinner's Savior, and are saluted with the loving assurance, "I have found a ransom; thy sins are forgiven thee; go in peace." Then the Holy Ghost opens to the soul God's love in Christ, which kindles in the believer's heart, and he is a new creature. The very love which the law of God requires springs up there, and forms a new element, a new life in his experience. "What the law could not do in that it was weak through the flesh," Christ has done for him, and "the righteousness of the law"—the right thing, in fact, which it requires—"is fulfilled in him" (Rom.

8 : 3, 4). Out of this fountain of love, his acts of obedience sweetly flow. He looks not for justification on the ground that his works are right, but on that of Christ's atonement alone; and his outward acts are expressive of his love to Jesus, which love, according to his measure of attainment and knowledge, will be coincident, in fact, with the love which the law demands.

Now, it is the grand policy of Satan, with men who desire to be righteous, to seduce them into a state of self-righteousness, to prevent their coming, as lost sinners, to the Redeemer, to receive the true righteousness as a free gift. He plays adroitly upon their sense of obligation to perform right deeds. He urges that it is most noble and wise; that God and man must alike be pleased with such consistency; that it will satisfy conscience and insure self-respect; that it is safe for time and hopeful for eternity; that it is profitable on general principles, at least, and can be followed by no disastrous consequences. Satan is a terribly urgent preacher of legal righteousness to those whom he sees disposed to inquire after the righteousness of faith. He would drive Sarah's children into the wilderness with Hagar. He would bewitch those who have begun in the Spirit (Gal. 3 : 1), subsequently to betake themselves to the law. A good brother, with an instructive experience on this subject, describes his exercises thus: "I thought I must obey the law, and went to Moses to make terms with him, and he at once knocked me down. I knew I deserved it, and did not complain. I prepared myself, and went again; and, with a severer blow, he brought me to the ground a second time. I was amazed, and entreated him to hear me. But he drove me from Sinai, and gave me no satisfaction. In my despair, I went to Calvary. There I found One who had pity on me, forgave my sins, and filled my heart with his love. I looked at him, and his healing mercy penetrated my whole being, and cured the malady within. Now, I went back to Moses to tell him what had happened. He smiled on me, shook my hand, and greeted me most lovingly; and he has never knocked me down since. I go by Calvary to Sinai, and all its thunders are silent."

What a rebuke was that of the self-righteousness of the Pharisees who had done so much, when Jesus set a little child before them, who had never offered one sacrifice, nor made one long prayer, and said *to them*, "Except ye be converted, and become as this little child, ye can not enter the kingdom of heaven." They did not know that the child's spirit of trust, dependence, and love was of more value than all their self-righteous services.

Are there not many in our churches who are saying, "Have we not eaten and drunk in thy presence? have we not prayed and labored in thy vineyard? have we not given our money to extend thy kingdom, and even done many wonderful works? Surely the door will not be shut against us." Would that they might escape this subtle device of the adversary, and make sure of the righteousness of faith.

Unconverted men, who are taken in this snare of the enemy, often affect to sneer at these discriminations. To such, let it be said that there is nothing in them peculiar to religion. If the breach and alienation were between a husband and wife, a parent and child, or between two personal friends, no outward acts, however fair in appearance toward third parties, would avail any thing. The offender must come back into loving and confiding relations to the offended, so that his conduct will be expressive of a true state of heart, or reconciliation is simply impossible. Until this is done, external deeds, no matter how plausible, can be, in the eye of the injured party, only hypocritical, and can only add insult to injury.

If any of this class of men are disposed to deny that God can have any controversy with those who hold that they are righteous before him, because they regard their own acts as righteous, their controversy is alike with the New Testament and with the common judgment of mankind.

CHAPTER XXVII.

SATAN'S EFFORTS TO CRIPPLE THE MINISTERS OF THE GOSPEL, AND RENDER THEIR PREACHING POWERLESS.

And he showed me Joshua, the high-priest, standing before the angel of the Lord, and Satan standing at his right hand to resist him.— *Zech.* 3:1.

In the context preceding the passage quoted, we have one of those prophetic visions, in which the Messiah appears to gather, enlarge, and bless his church. Jerusalem is measured, the Jews are brought back from their captivity in Babylon, the daughter of Zion is filled with praise and rejoicing, and many nations are gathered into the fold of the Divine Shepherd. Joshua, representing the priesthood, stands before the Lord of hosts, offering sacrifices upon his altar; and Satan also appears at his right hand — a most effective post — to resist him.

The vision is, doubtless, of New Testament times; and we are to regard Satan as now standing at the right hand of God's ministers, while engaged in their most holy functions, for the purpose of resisting them, and of defeating their best efforts to save men. That he has much success, who can doubt?

Upon no class of persons has God laid such responsibility as upon Christian ministers. None, perhaps, can do so much good or evil as they. Commissioned as God's embassadors to the world, Satan will, through them, strike at the whole race. If he can corrupt their hearts or their teachings, or misguide them in their life, it will go far toward the accomplishment of his dire purpose on the earth. None, therefore, more than they have need to be doubly armed against the foe.

Christ did not fail to make abundant provision for his ministers. When he bade them "go into all the world, and preach the gospel to every creature," he said, "Lo, I am with you always;" and before they should enter upon their great work, he pledged them the fulfillment of the "promise of the Father," by which they should be "endued with power from on high," and be introduced into the higher privileges and blessings of the New Testament, as distinguished from the Old. Waiting in Jerusalem till the day of Pentecost, they received the baptism of the Holy Ghost, and their lips were touched with heaven's fire. It is surely the New Covenant or Testament which furnishes the proper anointing for those who are called to preach the gospel. Between the Old and the New, the distinction is broad and vital. The Old "gendereth to bondage;" the New proclaims liberty: the Old opened the way into the outer tabernacle; the New rends the vail, and introduces the believer into the Holy of Holies: the Old could not purify the conscience; the New sprinkles it with clean water: the Old held forth the truth in letter and shadow; the New manifests its substance and spirit as an all-controlling, divine life in the soul itself: the Old had an infirm, human priesthood; the New has the Lord of glory himself for Priest, Mediator, and Surety.

Christ commanded his disciples, just before his ascension, not to depart from Jerusalem upon their mission to testify the gospel to the world, until he should be glorified, and the baptism of the Spirit should be given them. They waited, the Spirit descended, and the New Testament was fulfilled in them.

And now, dear brethren, does not this command to tarry in Jerusalem for "the promise of the Father," pertain to us as much as it did to those who first preached the gospel under the Spirit's dispensation? Vitally united to Christ by this baptism, we shall be able, in his strength, to do all things. Having this "unction from the Holy One," our ministry will be divinely authenticated. While our feet tread the paths of men, we shall walk with God, and enjoy a vivid realization of the truths we preach. Conscious, though we may be, of our infirmity and weakness, we shall know that his strength is made perfect, and abounds in our behalf. Ours will be an "earnest ministry," indeed, and our words will be as thunderbolts, or sunbeams, or drops of dew and honey, as our indwelling Immanuel shall please. Our faith will take hold of the highest and richest things of God's kingdom, and all the possibilities within us will be brought into the most vigorous use. There seems no good reason why the same unselfish devotion to Christ and the same burning zeal which characterized Paul should not be in us.

Without this heavenly anointing, we can doubtless preach; we can make the services of the sanctuary beautiful, impressive, and even solemn. Presenting the Divine Christ, only as in marble or on canvas, we may indeed stir the religious sensibilities and gain the "praise of men;" we may secure an outward prosperity, and "sell the pews," and meet the requirements of the church in her spiritual apathy; but can we obey the command, "Be ye clean, who bear the vessels of the Lord"? and can we habitually lead men to the spiritual apprehension of Christ? If we fail to move forward and gain the Spirit's teachings, must we not fall back into the legal dispensation, under the Old Covenant, and withhold from the people the liberty which Christ proclaims, and bring upon ourselves the fearful denunciations uttered by Ezekiel (Chap. 13, 14) against the prophets who "prophesy out of their own hearts," and " daub with untempered mortar"?

There are many ways in which Satan will strive to annihilate the moral power of our ministry.

1. First of all, he will, if possible, keep us from attaining the baptism of the Holy Spirit. To prevent this, no appliances will be left untried.

2. He will do his utmost to draw us into that state in which we shall so "seek the honor of men, and not the honor which cometh from God only," that the exercise of a living trust in Christ may be to us impossible. It is not easy to the natural man "to make ourselves of no reputation." The "old man" is proud and ambitious, and hates to go to the cross.

3. He will, if he can, induce us to rely upon our own wisdom and sufficiency — to "lean to our own understandings" more than is safe. Have we not been through the schools? Have we not studied the Bible, the canons of the church, and systems of doctrine, in dead languages and living ones? Have we not sat at the feet of the masters, and do we not know the truth? Subordinated to the Spirit's teachings, human learning is good; otherwise it will, in spiritual things, only mislead us. Paul's remark is as true now as when he made it, and of us as of himself — "Not that we are sufficient of ourselves to think any thing as of ourselves, but our sufficiency is of God." If we live not in the Spirit, we shall only promote a religion of the head — eminently satisfactory to our adversary — a religion which, one of our Unitarian journalists being judge, tends to "harden into skepticism, or flatten into formalism, or soften into sentimentalism, aestheticism, and such beautiful chants and prayers"!

4. Satan will strive to withhold us from sympathy

and real oneness with Christ in his spirit of self-sacrifice. He would make us unwilling to know our Master in the smallness of his salary; in his humility, coming, as he did, "not to be ministered unto but to minister;" in that benevolence which led him to love his enemies the more, the less they loved him, and to make their hatred to him a reason for using additional means to save them; and in that uncomplaining forbearance which he exhibited in the garden, before Pilate, under the crown of thorns, and upon the cross itself. Satan knows full well that the very beginning of a successful ministry lies in going to the cross with Christ, and there dying to all selfish, ambitious, and worldly ends. To prevent this sacrifice, this whole burnt offering, and the new life and power which succeed it, will be his most successful means of destroying our usefulness.

5. Satan will do his utmost to make our teaching promotive of righteousness by works rather than of faith. This is an age of activity, of ceaseless work, of outward demonstration. All are called upon to act, to give, to labor here and there in the service of God and man. It is in the natural heart to take credit for good deeds, and make a righteousness of them. An outward righteousness affords the most plausible way of shunning the cross, and yet gaining hope of heaven. From the identity of human nature, in all ages, there is a constant necessity of guarding

against the great error into which the Jews, in Christ's day, fell.

It is easy to ring changes on what men ought to do; but to bring home to them those influences which shall destroy all self-righteous hope, and open in their hearts fountains of love from which the vital current of true obedience shall spontaneously flow, requires that we be able ourselves to say with Paul, "I am crucified with Christ; nevertheless, I live; yet not I, but Christ liveth in me: and the life which I now live in the flesh, I live by the faith of the Son of God, who loved me and gave himself for me."

6. The salvation which the church needs is emphatically a present one. Here Satan is to be met; here the conflict rages; here the whole power of Christianity to bring the world to Christ should be manifested. If our ministrations can be construed to favor the idea that salvation is a future rather than a present thing, and mainly of another world, we may be sure that Satan will make the most of such a construction, and thus destroy much of our power in preaching Christ's gospel. With that view, we can surely do but little toward checking the too dominant influence of worldliness in the church.

I forbear to mention still other things of similar importance.

Dear brethren in the ministry, allow one of the least in the brotherhood to ask, Are we in the Spirit, and is our preaching in the demonstration of the

Spirit and with power? Do we speak with divine authority? Is the secret of the Lord with us, as we may and should have it? Are we in advance of the sacramental host, able to lead them up the mountain of the Lord, to the temple of his holiness? Can we conduct the people within the vail if we have not entered there ourselves?

The state of the world; the amazing sweep of influence which Satan has over men; the hastening forward of the grand events which the prophets foresaw in these later ages, and which are to herald the reign of Christ under a new heaven and on a new earth; the fact that so much depends upon the faithful exhibition of God's truth in the full power and authority of the Holy Ghost; and that such responsibilities are upon us as the embassadors of Christ, — all demand that we be furnished for our work as thoroughly as the gospel has provided that we may be; and that we so use our ministry that nothing of the glory of our Redeemer shall be lost through our neglect.

CHAPTER XXVIII.

THE GREAT FIGHT WITH AND VICTORY OVER SATAN; WITH A PASTOR'S SKETCH OF THE BATTLE SCENE

And the God of peace shall bruise Satan under your feet shortly. — *Rom.* 16 : 20.

IN the conflict with Satan, the saints are to be the conquerors. True, the victory is from God; but we are to stand upon the bruised head of the foe. The earnest Christian believer, girded with true heavenly might, is Guido's archangel, who, with the uplifted spear of God's double-edged Word, and with his foot upon the prostrate form of Satan, shall compel him to surrender.

To learn the way of fighting successfully the battle with Satan is a cardinal attainment. Upon this must depend the question, whether we are to spend our days in bondage or in liberty; whether we are to be the slaves of Satan, working his will, or the freemen of the Lord, rendering joyful and loving service to the Prince of Peace; whether we are to render a good or an evil report of the land of promise; whether we are to honor Christ or crucify him afresh.

When two great armies are arrayed against each other, the absorbing thought on both sides is, How shall we get advantage of the foe — how gain the victory? Nothing avails till the battle is won. So it should be with the church in her conflict with the principalities and powers of evil; so also with the individual disciple, who must, like David, be confronted with his Goliath, alone. How the victory can be surely won, we wish, with God's help, to illustrate.

But we must first see just where the issue between the contending parties lies. If we make a false issue with the enemy, we fail, of course; and he will, in this way, seek to outflank us if he can. We may seem to gain a battle when contending for the wrong thing, and have our bondage increased by the operation. Let us not be satisfied to take some outpost of the enemy, but rather march upon his capital.

Now, let it be considered, that, radically, the contest is not for the putting forth of certain external acts, as it might at first seem, but for maintaining the right state of the mind itself. If the true and righteous decision of the soul, in regard to any matter of outward duty, be inflexibly maintained, the outward act will certainly be put forth. The failure will be in giving up the decision. Nor is the contest to escape temptation. We can make no terms with the enemy by which he will agree to let us alone, unless we surrender unconditionally. Nor yet is the contest to retain a given state of the emotions. It is, indeed, agreeable to have an exultant state of the religious sensibility; but to have that, alike in the wilderness or in the promised land, in the garden or on the mount, may be neither possible nor desirable. God requires no such thing of us; nor did it appear in the experience of Christ himself.

The one great and essential issue is this: to hold the will true and loyal to the will of God. To swerve is defeat; to stand fast, victory.

The victorious element of our faith is just this voluntary one, which clings to Christ through storms and darkness; which goes with him without the camp bearing his reproach; which refuses to let the promise go, though the Angel of the Covenant himself seem to deny the blessing, and though the fulfillment be delayed, as in the case of Abraham for twenty-five long years, causing the soul to stagger under the severity of the trial; which insists upon the divine faithfulness, although it seem to the mind that there is no possible way in which the promise can be fulfilled; and which will not shrink from the agony of the garden, nor from the shameful death of the cross. To such a faith, indeed, "nothing is impossible;" and it insures the complete victory over Satan and every foe.

Remembering that the great decisive battle turns upon this one point, the reader is invited to behold the conflict and the victory, in the following

Sketch

Of the experience of the pastor referred to in a previous chapter. He had, as there shown, come to the knowledge of Christ, as a present and all-sufficient

Redeemer. God had revealed his Son in him, in a sense before unknown. The manifestation was precious beyond the power of language to describe. Christ and the Father had "come unto him to make their abode with him." His soul seemed quickened with the very life of God, and the promise, "Because I live, ye shall live also," was now his own by the sealing of the Spirit. The branch had come to abide in that Vine whose living currents carry healing whithersoever they flow. The joy was unutterable. Love filled his whole being, and overflowed in every direction toward God and all his creatures. Peace was, literally, like a river, and the righteousness of Christ, in him, like the waves of the sea. Faith reached the point of complete rest, of quietness and unwavering assurance. To love enemies, for Christ's sake, was as easy as to love friends; to bear the reproach of Jesus was a conscious pleasure; to fill up what was lacking in his sufferings, a sweet privilege. O, how excellent was this knowledge of God! It was inspiring and life-giving indeed. The Bible was all luminous with the life and love of Jesus. The deep things of God rose to the surface. It was as if the Infinite One were communing with the soul, face to face, and the response was ready, "Through Christ who strengtheneth me," thus, "I can do all things," "bear all things," for in him is everlasting strength. For weeks, this excellent glory filled and satisfied his entire nature.

But at length the scene was changed. The fountain of these living waters seemed dry. The light was gone, the glory had disappeared, and the consciousness of a present Savior was wholly wanting. The Father and Son seemed to have withdrawn from their abode in the temple within. The Word was silent and dark. The promises were there, but their streams of blessing would not flow. Joy was turned to sadness. Love, from a glowing and intense emotion, had come to be only a voluntary preference. All the waves and billows were driving around and upon the soul.

Amazed and startled, the then student cried unto God, "Lord, why is this? Have I sinned? Have I grieved thy Spirit? What shall I do? which way turn?" The difficulty was made all the worse that no immediate answer came. The heart was searched for an Achan, but nothing believed to be wrong was detected. Its language was, "Sooner let me die than sin." The whole soul was in agony at such a state of things. To one older in the faith of a present Redeemer, the case was stated, who said, "*It is temptation; but cling to Jesus, and he will give you a glorious deliverance. It is for the trial of your faith. Satan desires to have you, and sift you as wheat; but stay yourself directly upon the promise, and victory is sure!*"

Now the battle was inaugurated. Satan would, if possible, force the agonized disciple to give up Christ as a present and almighty Savior, and to yield the conflict, under the idea that salvation was only a future and distant thing. Will the victory come? was the question. There stood the promise, confirmed by the immutable oath of the Promiser; but, as yet, it seemed only words — powerless words. The student's own strength was literally nothing. It seemed to him that a gossamer thread would better serve the purpose of a ship's cable, than his own strength would serve him in that battle with the powers of darkness. He said in his heart, "I anchor myself to the promise, 'My grace is sufficient for thee,' and looking unto Jesus by faith, I will sit at his feet and await the result."

Satan was mad, and at once opened all his batteries upon the stripling believer. The shell and steel-pointed shot flew faster than they could be counted. It seemed as if hell were let loose upon him, to assault him, at every point, in his nature and character. The adversary stole the thunders of Sinai, and fought his antagonist with the terrors of the law. All manner of vile suggestions and corrupting thoughts were paraded before the eye of the imagination. The catalogue of his old sins was unrolled before his memory, and they were made to thunder with condemnation and wrath, as if they had never been forgiven. The old sore spots, which mercy had healed up, were torn open anew, and reinflamed with conviction. Hebrews 6: 4–8, was adroitly urged by the adversary to extinguish hope and initiate a reign of fear and terror. The agony of the mind became almost insupportable. The deep cry of the young man was, "My God, my God, why hast thou forsaken me!" He could only lie upon his couch and groan in anguish of spirit; and yet his soul said, "To go to the cross, even in this horror of darkness and conflict, is better than to yield." For days, the battle continued to grow fiercer and more terrible, till his soul began almost to stagger and tremble for the result.

At length the Spirit came near, and entered into communion with the suffering disciple, and showed him where he was. The smoke of the battle cleared away, and it was given him to see, that, up to that point, he had not yielded. His will had remained firm. His moral position seemed to him to be well illustrated by a bridge thrown across a rapid stream, familiar to him in his boyhood. A firm stone abutment stood in the middle of the river, successfully resisting and turning aside the rushing waters, and sustaining the structure above. So, by God's grace, his will yet *stood*. But it was clear that Satan was pouring out his powerful spirit upon him, and that the flood of temptation was yet rising like the river in a spring freshet; and then the question forced upon the mind, in this review, was, Will not the mad flood rise above the pier, carry away the bridge above, and finally bring down the abutment? Just at that juncture, when the mind was querying whether the temptation would not be *greater than it could bear*, the Holy Ghost opened and sealed these words of promise on the waiting heart: "There hath no temptation taken you but such as is common to man; but God is faithful, who will not suffer you to be tempted *above that ye are able*, but will, with the temptation, make a way to escape, that ye may be able to bear it." The victory was won, the enemy completely routed. It could not have been more perfect if the foe had been annihilated before the victor's eye.

For the first time, in a seven years' Christian life, that disciple had learned to fight the good fight, and gain the victory of faith in a present, almighty Redeemer. It seemed to him as if he leaped, soul and body, in his exultation, to the ceiling of his room; and such expressions as these came spontaneously from his lips: "Now, Satan, I know you, and how to triumph over you;" "Glory to God, I am more than conqueror through Him who has loved me;" "This lesson is worth to me a thousand worlds;" "The victory of Wellington over Napoleon was nothing to this;" "Thanksgiving and praise be unto Jesus, the Prince and Deliverer." The joy, the peace, and the glory which had been withdrawn for this trial of faith, all returned with doubly enhanced richness and fullness. The lessons from this victory were numerous and invaluable.

Afterward, when temptation came, and faith was

to be tried, as in the fire, the battle was easily fought. The soul settled itself down upon the promise, and waited patiently for the Deliverer, who was sure to come. The teachings of the Spirit in these conflicts were valuable, and furnished material wherewith to comfort the church of God in his future ministry.

On one occasion afterward, this young man went through an experience of trial and victory, the narration of which may be of service to others tried in like way. The peculiarity of the trial was *its long continuance.* The soul became tired with waiting, and wondered why the Deliverer did not appear. The very length of the temptation became a source, at last, of great uneasiness. Why was it so? He seemed to himself to bear it patiently, and knew not why the Lord delayed his coming. This long delay brought a severe strain upon the mind.

At length, a good Scotch brother, who well knew the wiles and the depths of Satan, was showing, in his sermon, how the adversary sometimes tries to break the hold of the will upon Christ by a *long, persistent pressure of temptation upon it.* It was as if he had set a siege about the soul to starve it into surrender. He told the following story in illustration: An old Scotch baron was attacked by his enemy, who encamped before his gates, and would allow no provisions to enter them. He continued the siege long enough to have exhausted the supplies within, but there were no signs of capitulation. Weeks and months passed away, and yet no surrender. After a long time, the besieger was surprised, one morning, to see a long line of fish, fresh from the sea, hung over the wall; as much as to say, "We can feed you; and surely you can not starve us out, so long as there are fish in the sea, for we have an underground connection with it, and the supply is exhaustless!" "So," said the preacher, "Satan may besiege our gates, but he can never compel us to surrender, for our food comes, not through the gates, but from above, and through channels invisible to his eye; and the living Bread of Life, which is inexhaustible, is within the gates. No matter how long the siege, we need not fear." And thus, a precious way of escape was opened to our long-tried student.

Mrs. Hester Ann Rogers so well learned this great lesson of overcoming by faith, that she finally gave herself little or no concern about temptation. She seemed able, as it were, to feel the shadow of a coming trial before it reached her, and, with a strong and beautiful faith, she would humbly and confidently say to the great Deliverer, "Lord, see thou to that," and the victory was sure to come. And why not?

Christ fights the battle with us; he even makes it his own (2 Chron. 20 : 15); and why should we not expect of him always to give us a decisive and triumphant victory? Let us not limit the Holy One of Israel, who can make lice, and flies, and frogs stronger for us than Pharaoh can be against us.

By the successful fighting, for a season, of the "good fight of faith," by the knowledge and strength gained in the process, temptation may ere long cease seriously to disturb us. As a means of greater purity and growth, it may even, if God so please, be quite welcome. Our victory will be permanent. Indeed our own agency may come to be so swallowed up in Christ, our interests so absolutely one with his, that we shall not practically know ourselves except as being in him, or recognize any other agency than his in the work of our salvation. We may gain the moral position of Paul, and know nothing but Christ and him crucified.

The true and earnest Christian shall be more than a conqueror. His triumph over Satan shall be so much beyond a bare victory, that that enemy himself shall be made a most effective instrument in developing, in minute and beautiful proportions on the believer's heart, that very image of the Lord Jesus which he sought to damage or destroy. He shall learn, by a most blessed experience, the fact that God overrules even the devices of Satan, as well as all other forms of evil, to the upbuilding in faith and holiness of those who believe in him. Let not the believer, then, fear the conflict. Soon, standing upon the crystal sea, with the "harp of God" in his hand, he shall sing the conqueror's song, and wear the conqueror's crown.

www.ingramcontent.com/pod-product-compliance
Lightning Source LLC
Chambersburg PA
CBHW022049230426
43672CB00008B/1114